George Keate

Sketches From Nature

Taken, And Coloured, in a Journey to Margate (Volume 2)

George Keate

Sketches From Nature
Taken, And Coloured, in a Journey to Margate (Volume 2)

ISBN/EAN: 9783744743716

Printed in Europe, USA, Canada, Australia, Japan

Cover: Foto ©Thomas Meinert / pixelio.de

More available books at **www.hansebooks.com**

SKETCHES

FROM

NATURE;

TAKEN, AND COLOURED, IN A

JOURNEY TO MARGATE.

PUBLISHED FROM THE

ORIGINAL DESIGNS.

BY GEORGE KEATE, Esq.

VOL. II.

LONDON:

PRINTED FOR J. DODSLEY, PALL-MALL.

M.DCC.LXXIX.

SKETCHES

FROM

NATURE.

THE APOLOGY.

IT is much eafier to read a book, than to write one;—and fhould any fkeptical gentleman doubt this propofition, I wifh, for his own fatisfaction, he would make the experiment.

—A reader may, either with or without his fpectacles, as he and his eyes can fettle it, travel through a volume juft at what rate he pleafes, or ftop fhort the inftant that he finds

his

his road unentertaining; but a poor devil of an author muſt go on with the utmoſt caution,—looking backwards, and forwards, and ſideways, and endways—and hath buſineſs enough on his hands, to keep every thing tight together, that his work doth not tumble to pieces.—He is in truth, only the reader's pioneer, to clear all obſtructions, open his views, and render his way cheerful.—

As every advantage ſeems to be thrown on the reader's ſide, I muſt, as an author, contend, that there are ſome indulgences due to us.—I do not preſume to hint, that we have the privilege of taking a nap, becauſe our reader hath; on the contrary, it is incumbent on us to keep his eyes open as long as poſſible, as his ſleep may be death to us;—but ſurely, while

we

we are bufied in entertaining him, we may be allowed a little recreation ourfelves,—and if a delicious mea-dow, or a tempting piece of green-fward, lies by the road-fide, what literary code is there, to prohibit our taking a canter over it, though it lie out of the *ftraight line* of our jour-ney ?—For my own part, whenever the old horfe I ride hath a mind for a frifk, either to the right, or the left, I feel that I muft, and will, in-dulge his humour, in fpite of all the canons of criticifm.—As long as it is natural, they may fire and welcome.—

—Now *ftraight lines* are, and ever were, my averfion ; — my writing-mafter could never tempt me when a child, to ufe them ;—they may ferve admirably well for rulers—walking-fticks—mafts—or may-poles, — but

the

the *line of beauty* difavows them.—
The FRENCH, it is true, lay out their
roads by them, becaufe their notions
of liberty and property, allow them
to cut through any thing,—but ours
in this country, being more delicate
on the fubjeĉt, it is by many curves
—and windings—and pleafant turn-
ings, that we get from town to town.
—In fhort, *ftraight lines* are now ab-
folutely exploded,—they are not found
to lead to the preferments of the
world;—nor do hereditary virtues, or
fortunes, run any longer in them!—
Every road from BERWICK upon
TWEED to PENZANCE, is *zig-zag*—
every modern walk and plantation,
zig-zag,—every avenue about court,
zig-zag,—and fo too are all our ideas;
—nay, and what is much to be lamented, fo are all our lives too.—
—And

[5]

—And this is that which frets their reverences so much ; and will, to the end of time, furnish us with new volumes of sermons.——

. ——However disgusting to the eye the *straight line* may appear, yet any digreffion from it, which, after a little curve, reverts into it; becomes a pleafing form;—and fhould digreffions interfect the *straight line* on the other fide alfo, the whole united, takes nearly the figure of MERCURY's *Caduceus*, which is indifputably the true *ferpentine*, and the fineft model to write by;—and befides, being perfectly *antique*, you had better go to bed, be you who you will, than open your mouth againft it.——

——Having faid thus much in fupport of an author's privilege, and at the fame time, in favor of *occafional*

B 3 *digreffions,*

digreſſions, not only in my own work,—
but in any work,—or in every work,
—I beſeech the reader, ſhould he
chance to ſee me ſet off on a ſudden,
that he would not halloo after me,
but that he will conclude, I am in pur-
ſuit of ſomething for his ſervice,—
and conſider that every writer knows,
or ſhould know, his way home, and
is bound to take care of his own
neck.—

—And now, COURTEOUS READER,
let us ſet forward once more together.
—If thou really haſt a claim to the
appellation I have given thee, thou
art juſt the perſon I am looking for,
whenever I ſet pen to paper:—but if,
on the contrary, thou haſt refined
away thy power of being pleaſed;—
if thou canſt ſacrifice thy feelings
to rules,—and be out of humour at
every

every little thing that may happen
amifs—e'en let us feparate the firft
fhort turning we come to; for I would
not travel with thee, though thou
fhouldft defray my expences to the
world's end.—

THE HOY.

I WISH, from my heart, I had given it the gentleman, thought I !—as a perfon who fat next to me at LANG-FORD's, was chaffering for a book, which he wifhed for, in a lot of feveral I had juft bought,—for whilft he was peftering me about proportioning the purchafe money, I inattentively miffed another lot that foon followed, which was a very fcarce SPANISH romance, I had long been in queft of, and had come purpofely to buy; which was fnapped up by a *book-fancier*, merely on account of its fcarcity, for he knew not a word of the language it was wrote in.—

I am at this inftant almoft in the fame fituation; for while I have been

capitulating

capitulating with the reader,—or as the law would term it, settling articles of agreement with him, here is the devil and all to do in MARGATE;—half a dozen men tied up in facks, and hopping for a pig—three jack-affes running for a CHESHIRE cheefe,—and a fmock-race on the fands,—and all the world there,—whilft the prize, decorated with ribbands, is carried in proceffion on a pole, like a popifh relique.—Every circumftance of life is proportionate;—the *Golden Pippin* on Mount IDA did not more agitate the three *Celeftial* competitors, than this little object did our three *terreftrial* ones here.—Happy fhe who conquers! —as the lafs with a fhift to her back, ftands a far better chance for prefer- ment, than fhe who has none.—And fee the victrix has it flipped over her

running

running dreſs, and marches off tri-
umphant,—with a drum before her
—and a mob at her heels!—

But this is not half the buſtle; for
two Hoys are juſt arrived from London, their decks covered with new
comers, and all Margate running
down to the *Pier-head* to ſee them
land.—I doubt whether I am ſtout
enough to run too,—but I will be
amongſt them as faſt as I can walk.—
If I lean over this rail, I ſhall ſee them
all come aſhore.—

Mercy on me !—I think the whole
city of London is aboard of ſhip !—
ſix !—eight !—ten !—twenty !—thirty !
fifty !—ſeventy !—I can never go on
reckoning at this rate.—What !—are
all the ſhops ſhut up ?—

—Or have you been all *bit*, good
people ?—

—Or

—Or are you come here to be *bit?*
— The wind has been dreadfully
againſt you the whole way !—

—Why, as faſt as the boats fill,
the deck is covered again with new
faces that riſe out of the hold !—
There is no end of it !—I will poſitively
count no more.—Nay, ladies, you
need not ſay how ſick you have been,
—your looks will vouch for you.—
A tedious paſſage,—high ſea,—all
the pumps continually going,—and
no room to ſtir, even to the ſhip's
ſide, on neceſſary calls—it is mon-
ſtrouſly inconvenient !—but it is *a party
of pleaſure,* and that is enough.—

Ha !—What is your Worſhip come
down too?—and Madam ?—and little Miſs ?—pray take care how you
get up the ſteps.—All for the water,
I ſuppoſe ?—

Give

‘ Give that fat lady, in the *Brunf-wick*, your arm, my lad ;—don't you fee how lame fhe is ?—poor foul !—fcarce a leg to ftand on.—If the fea can fet her upright, it muft work a miracle !—

Confidering the freight, and the live ftock, thefe veffels have brought down, I am in aftonifhment where they could ftow fo many odd bundles, and bandboxes befides.—Why. there is two at leaft to every paffenger,—filled, no doubt, with all the. neweft-fafhioned curls, — pompoons —caps,—and apologies for caps.—We fhall certainly have a general review of them at MITCHENER's next Ball,—and the heads they belong to—and the people who own the heads.—

But now all the world is fcampering another way after two coaches and

and four, and three poft-chaifes;—
butchers,—bakers,—hair-dreffers,—
and milliners,—running in a cloud of
duft at their fide; and all the bathers
elbowing each other, and contending
for the honour of ducking the company who are in them.—

—The more the merrier, if you
can but find beds to creep into.—Well,
—it is a mighty pleafant thing to be
on one's travels,—and nothing fo fafhionable—for fick, or well, no body
ftays at home.—

I am glad, however, that I have
got the ftart of fome of you, and am
not juft fetting out on mine.—

THE

THE RIDE.

I GROW weary of the traveller, who pefters one with every thing he fees; carrying his pen and ink, like an *excifeman*, at his button-hole, to minute down his obfervations on every gutter he croffes. — There is fcarcely any confiderable object, between SHOOTER's HILL and MOUNT ÆTNA, which hath not been defcribed, well, or ill, by fome author or other; —a hint ftrong enough to determine me to defcribe nothing profeffedly,— but to travel and write in my own way, which I can demonftrate to be the very beft way yet hit on, and attended with the leaft fatigue to thofe who travel with one.

—Whoever gives long, or laboured defcriptions,

3

descriptions, loads his reader with a quantity of *matter of fact* which lies a dead weight on his head, as he goes on, and which many indeed have not a head to bear;—but by offering him no more than SKETCHES, his imagination (should the out-lines be judiciously taken) is complimented, and set at work; busied to fill up all the lights and shades, and give every part its true tone of colouring.—

Wherever I turn my eye, NATURE is the great object it fixes on.—I catch all the little incidents she throws in my way,—whether they arise from her *silent scenes* that solicit our admiration, or from her *active ones* that interest our passions.—This steady attention to all her movements, renders my walks and my rides luxurious;—I contemplate with delight the simplicity

plicity

plicity of the cottager, and all the domeſtic occurrences of artleſs life— not a ſhell, or a ſea-weed, that the wave throws on the ſhore; not a wild flower that illumines the corn-field, nor a butterfly that flutters acroſs my horſe's head, but awakens ſome agreeable idea in my mind.——

LA PIERRE when he is riding with me, often interrupts me with his officious care; and conceives I am not well when I ſtop ſhort on a ſudden, to muſe over any of theſe trivial circumſtances.——He has ſo much *naïveté* and good humour, that one cannot be diſpleaſed with him; and too much of the Frenchman to comprehend what it is that engages me.——The *je ne vois rien,* which is his common reply, may come as naturally from the mouth of many of my readers, who

who are daily treading under foot, or
paffing by unnoticed, the little objects which contribute to my entertainment.——

The reafon is, that their eyes are
looking another way.——

Ah! voilà mon païs! cries LA PIERRE,
with an emphafis that fhewed the ex-
clamation was warm from his heart.
——So I knew *which way his eyes were
looking*——for I was juft then riding in
a moft lovely evening, on that beautiful terrace that runs from the NORTH
FORELAND, to BROAD STAIRS, with
the FRENCH coaft ftretched in full view
before me.——My mind kindled with
delight, at the fight of the azure ex-
panfe of waters beneath me, and the
many bufy white fails that were cut-
ting their way acrofs it.——The ra-
diance of the fetting fun defcending

VOL. II.   C   in

in flames of gold, gave a glow to every thing around—the inmoft receffes of my breaft felt its warmth.—

I wonder, fays La Pierre, what they are doing juft now at Amiens?——

—Why undoubtedly clofing fuch a day as this with a dance.—

—And dancing at Paris,—and at Lyons,—and in the plains of Languedoc — and along the fhore of Marseille—and in the Moon too, for any thing we know to the contrary.—

Vive la joie—a cheerful heart can never be a bad one!—

—The deuce take this poor fellow's inquifitivenefs, for ftarting up all thefe ideas, for now that he has got me as far as Marseille, I am in the midft of all their *baftides* and *orangeries*, and all the glitter and per-

7   fume

fume of that enchanting coaft!—and
I am dancing with them, under their
mulberry-trees, to the tabour and
pipe;—and my ear is full of their little
fprightly airs,—and my mind crowded with a thoufand occurrences that
befell me there.—

— Well, *vive la joie encore*;—
and as memory, fays I, can ride poft
at this rate, I'll often have a peep at
you, and dance with you again, and
again.—

Thou art a happy, lively, fenfible
people!—Thy country teems with
men of genius, who cultivate thofe
arts which embellifh life; and that
eafe of manners which fweetens fociety!—when nature hath placed us
fo near each other, I grieve we fhould
be fo frequently foes!—

A plague on the paltry interefts of

C 2   the

the world!—that the catching a little fish in another quarter of the globe,
or a conteft for a little dominion, in
a land of favages, fhould arm nation
againſt nation,—make them fufpend
all the graces of courtefy,—and in-
volve fuch legions of wretches in the
complicated miferies of war !—

THE

THE reflected light from the white cliffs of FRANCE, on which my eyes were fixed, made them appear to prefs forward on my fight; and while my imagination was taking a frifk from the STREIGHTS OF DOVER, to the MEDITERRANEAN, and dropping a figh, over political neceffity—I found I had thrown the reins of my horfe on his neck, who had taken the advantage of my inattention, to pick up a little clover that grew by the way-fide.——

——Nay,—if it be thy will, old companion, fays I, e'en take the other bite;—the farmer will be never the poorer for the mouthful thou fhalt carry away;—did he know thy good

C 3 quali-

qualities, he would let thee eat thy fill.—

—I will not interrupt thy pleafurable moments,—fo prithee feed on.— Long have I wifhed an occafion to record thy deferts, thou faithful old fervant!—It now prefents itfelf,— and thou fhalt have a page in my book, though it provoke the fneer of the critic.—It is thy due, for thou haft given me health.—Full many a year haft thou journeyed with me, through the uneven ways of the world! —We have tugged up many a fteep hill, and borne the buffet of the tempeft together!—I have had the labours of thy youth, and thy age hath a claim on me, which, while I have fixpence in my pocket, I dare not refufe.—

—Thou fhalt not, when thy ftrength

is

is exhaufted, be configned to poverty and toil!—or, as thou paffeft by my door, lafhed on by fome unfeeling owner, look at me with the fevere eye of reproach!—

—Had THAT HAND, which fafhioned us both, endued thy fpecies with the faculty of fpeech, in what bitternefs of heart would they complain of the ingratitude of ours!—

—In the wide extent of the animal reign, there fcarce exifts an object from which man may not borrow fome ufeful hint;—thou, my trufty friend, haft offered me no inconfiderable one;—thou never aimed to appear what thou waft not;—a fteady walk, or a cheerful trot, was all thou attempted,—nay, perhaps it was as much as thy mafter himfelf afpired to; —and when remembrance fhall be

weighing

weighing thy merits, the scale shall turn in thy favor, when I reflect, that thou scorned to desert the path of *nature* for the perilous one of *affecta-tion!*—

—Is it not owing to this error, that so many *nags,* whom Providence had destined for the *plough,* or the *shaft,* are daily provoking *a horse-laugh* in the world, by awkwardly striving to imitate the graces of the *turf,* or the caprioles of the *manage?*

THE STORY OF MARIANNE.

A S I devoted moſt of my after-
noons to CLERMONT, and his
family,—on calling in, this evening, I
found AMELIA had ſent MARIANNE
to the rooms, with ſome young people of her acquaintance.—I have almoſt been compelled, ſays ſhe, to force
her out ;—ſhe loves retirement much
more than I wiſh her to do—I think
her ſpirits, though commonly very
good, require ſometimes the relaxa-
tion of public ſcenes, to divert them
from the recollection of domeſtic
events, which are every now and then
painful to her.—And yet, if it is not
to accompany me, it is with the utmoſt difficulty, I can prevail on her
to mix in the world.

—I be-

—I believe, in general, said I, Madam, that young and ingenuous minds, whose expectations of it have been somewhat deceived, are not easily brought to be on good terms with it again :—the hope of youth is ardent, and its sensibility proportionably acute.—

—I fear, indeed, returned AMELIA, that such have been her impressions; and as she has a heart fashioned for all the virtues of society, I most earnestly wish to see them effaced.—I know she entertains the highest opinion of you, and is much flattered by the attention you have shewn her;—a few hints therefore from you, when opportunity offers, would, I am persuaded, have great weight with her;—and as we are now alone, if my brother will take up the news-paper,
and

and fufpend his party for half an hour, I will add a few particulars to the general idea I have given you before, of her fituation; and fhe fhall know from me, that you are apprized of the whole.—

—When my much-loved friend, her mother, died, fhe left only two children, — MARIANNE, who had then juft compleated her fixteenth year, and her brother EDMUND, who was three-and-twenty;—but fo oppofite were their characters, that no one who knew them intimately, could have fuppofed they fprang from the fame parents.—She, all tendernefs and undiffimulated nature;—he, a compound of artifice, and meannefs,—guiding every action by avarice and intereft, but varnifhing his deportment with fo

much

much plaufibility, that his hypocrify not only deceived the world into
a favourable opinion of him, but impofed on the heart of his fifter, even
though fhe fometimes doubted his
conduct.

Though the father furvived his
lady near four years, yet her lofs affected him fo deeply, that his health
began to decline apace.—EDMUND
had fo induftrioufly practifed on him,
all his affumed powers to pleafe, and
was befides on fuch excellent terms
with himfelf, that he doubted not but
his merits would inevitably intitle him
to the whole inheritance of his father's eftate ;—and as a fifter was a
very inconfiderable object in a family,
he conceived the trifling portion which
would be allotted her, he might be
eafily

eafily able to pay off, by his profeffion at the bar, which began now to
be profitable to him.

While EDMUND's vanity was nourifh-
ing thefe flattering ideas, the conduct
of MARIANNE towards her father, was
fuch as is the natural refult of the
trueft affection and duty.—Whether
his penetration ever contrafted the
real characters of his two children,
we know not—he appeared to teftify
an equal regard to both;—but in the
difpofition of his affairs, which was
communicated to no one till his death,
he acted differently from the generality of parents; who fuffer their
pride totally to fubdue the feelings of
nature, when, to aggrandize one child,
they too often leave all the reft who
have been equally the objects of their
tendernefs, either in a ftate of depen-
dance,

dance, or bequeath them such a dis-
proportionate provision, as they can
but with the utmost difficulty, subsist
on—a conduct, which, however it
may be influenced by political views,
hath ever appeared to be irreconcile-
able with parental tenderness.—

On my conscience, sister, says CLER-
MONT (taking his eyes from the news-
paper he was reading) you argue this
matter admirably well ! — You will
have all the younger children in the
nation of the same opinion !—

—Prithee, brother, do not disturb
my story.—

—Do not make it longer then than
the *Evening-post*,—for I must have my
party at back-gammon.—

THE

THE STORY OF MARIANNE.

IMMEDIATELY on the father's death, refumed AMELIA—who had never even hinted to his children, the teftamentary difpofition he had made —EDMUND privately opened his will, and to his great aftonifhment, found his father had bequeathed the fum of ten thoufand pounds to MARIANNE, chargeable on his eftate, which was valued at about twenty-three thoufand,—leaving his fon the eftate, together with the fum of two thoufand pounds, which he had in money.—

This fo thoroughly difconcerted EDMUND's views, that, availing himfelf of a declaration dropped from his fifter, that fhe never had heard her father mention a will; he conceived
the

the idea of concealing this, he had found; and it was prefumed in the family that there actually exifted none; —but a duplicate having been depofited by the father, in the hands of a friend, who was gone to fettle fome affairs at LISBON, at his return three months after, underftanding that his old acquaintance was deceafed during his abfence, he waited on the family with the counterpart, that had been entrufted to his care.—

This circumftance threw EDMUND into fuch a confternation, as wanted an explanation, to thofe who were witneffes of it; though the real caufe was fometime after conjectured, when the other part of the will (to which there was a reference on the cover of the duplicate) was produced by ED-MUND, and pretended to be found very

2   obfcurely

obfcurely mixed, among fome infig-
nificant papers of his father's.

MARIANNE had too much penetration not to be ftartled at this accident;—it led her to fufpicions not
very favourable to her brother,—but
it offered her a noble and unexpected
independency; and gave a heart fo
full of fenfibility as her's, the higheft
joy; as it was the ftrongeft teftimony
of her father's having approved the
duty and affection fhe had fhewn
him.—

EDMUND began now to call in aid,
that hypocrify, of which he was fo
much mafter;—he affected to veil his
difappointment with great good humour,—he paid every poffible attention to his fifter; and often expreffed
his fatisfaction, at the provifion his
father had made for her.—At other

VOL. II. D times,

times, when he found opportunities that were favourable, he would put on a dejected air,—lament the concern he felt to part with the family eftate, —which he acquainted her he muft be under the neceffity of doing, from his inability to keep it up, with fuch a heavy charge as her fortune was, on it ; which infinitely exceeded in proportion, the ufual difpofitions made to daughters,—that he had befides contracted feveral large debts in his father's life-time, which would overfhadow all his future purfuits,—and in conclufion, that he faw no method by which he could be extricated from the many difficulties that preffed him, unlefs MARIANNE would, from her affection to him, relinquifh part of her claim.—He added, that no one was fo near to her, as himfelf,—nor did his
modefty

modefty fcruple to hint, that half the fum his father had bequeathed her, would command whatever a reafonable woman could require.——

MARIANNE, who knew that the exact parfimony which directed ED-MUND's conduct, by no means tallied with the declaration he had made concerning his private incumbrances, often felt the awkwardnefs of her fituation;—it ftartled—it embarraffed her;—and her benevolence, ever more awake than her caution, prompted her one day, when he had renewed the fame fubject, to fay, in general terms, that a brother's happinefs could not but influence hers,—that the ge-nerofity of her father had been his own free act, and till the production of his will, totally unknown to her,—and that, fhould any event in life

arife

arife, in which she could be inftrumen-
tal to his welfare, he might reft fa-
tisfied, she should retain a difpofition
of being fo.——

——Avarice often defeats its own defigns, by purfuing them with an ill-
judged ardour!——this was Edmund's
cafe,——who, conceiving that the kind
avowal of his fifter would precipitate
her into his ftratagem, thought it now
a favourable crifis to produce a deed
that he had prepared;—— whereby,
from motives of affection, she agreed,
that in cafe his affairs should require
it, to accept of five thoufand pounds
for her fortune, in lieu of the ten
thoufand, bequeathed her by her father;——he affected indeed to give a
plaufible colour to the propofal, by
faying, that it refted on events very
remote—that moft probably he never

3   should

fhould ftand in need of it,—but only wifhed that the deed fhould remain as *a mark of love* between them.—

MARIANNE inftantly faw through the defign, and turned pale at the idea of its bafenefs;—fhe concealed however, in fome meafure, her indignation; and with as much compofure as fhe could fummon, told EDMUND, that his propofal was beyond her power to gratify;—and though you dignify it, fays fhe, with the appellation of *a mark of love*, yet believe me, brother, it is not only unworthy of you, but unworthy of me—it betrays a total diffidence in my honour, by endeavouring to fetter, with the obligations of law, any act of affection which ought only to be the refult of inclination,—nor fhould *compulfion*

ever

ever effect that in my heart, which *choice* could not decide.——

EDMUND endeavoured to explain away the ill appearance of his defign, by wifhing her to think, it was only in confequence of the good intentions which fhe had teftified towards him ;——and MARIANNE retiring, left him in full poffeffion of thofe feelings, which arife from the mifcarriage and detection of a difhonourable action.——

As my young friend had been trained up by her deceafed mother, to look on me with the moft affectionate regard, fhe had accuftomed herfelf, on every occafion, to open her heart to me without referve.——I perceived how much it was diftreffed by her brother's conduct; and having,

immediately

immediately on her father's death, invited her to the protection of my roof, I now saw many reasons to insist on her accepting it without delay; —which she accordingly soon did,—preserving at the same time, all those appearances, which we both of us wished should still be maintained.

—I will not dwell longer on a character which can only afford pain to a man of your turn of mind; let me only add, that Edmund had free access to my house whenever he pleased, and continued to be received, if not with confidence, yet always with attention;—till an event arose, which of necessity precluded him from any future intercourse with us.

—Marianne's father had testified a particular regard to a young man of good family, of the name of Ster-

LING,

LING, with fome of whofe relations, he had been much connected; he had alfo fufficient intereft to introduce him fo fortunately into the fervice of·the EAST INDIA *Company,* that by his abilities and good conduct, he was appointed to the command of a fhip, at a much earlier period than young men in general attain fuch promotion; and had, by the time her father died, made one voyage as captain, with great credit and advantage to himfelf, and was on his return from his fecond.——

The grateful fenfe he ever retained of her father's fervices, made Captain STERLING, when at home, a frequent vifitor at the houfe; and it was about feven months before he returned from his fecond voyage, that he loft his friend and benefactor.——As his fa-

mily

mily and mine, had alſo enjoyed a long intimacy, he was accuſtomed to call on me often; but I found his vi-ſits now were more than uſually re-peated; and ſoon perceived there was a perſon under my roof, that attracted him more ſtrongly than myſelf;—I thought alſo, that the attachment was apparently reciprocal on the part of my young friend,—and I ſaw it with infinite pleaſure—as I ſincerely wiſhed an union, which on both ſides bid ſo fair for happineſs.

Captain STERLING was about nine years older than MARIANNE; his fi-gure was pleaſing and manly,—he poſſeſſed great delicacy of ſentiment;—and was one who governed his life by the principles of the niceſt honour;—he was as much enamoured of her mind, as of her perſon,—and his love

was

was poffibly heightened by the idea of her being the daughter of a friend, whofe kind offices he ever recollected with the warmeft gratitude.——

Her affection was founded on a bafis equally firm :——She had known him long ;——fhe refpected the amiablenefs of his character,——admired his cheerful, open temper,——and regarded him as a protector and companion, with whom fhe could, hand in hand, fecurely tread the paths of future life.——It was a contract, uncontaminated on either fide by intereft ;——and as their wills depended on themfelves, they had nothing but their own hearts to confult.——

——There was only one obftacle, which prevented the immediate completion of their wifhes:——The reputation that Captain STERLING had acquired

quired among the *Directors*, had procured him foon after his return, a no-
mination to go out to MADRASS and
CHINA, which is generally regarded as
the moft lucrative ftation to be named
to,—and he was appointed to command
the INGOT, efteemed the fineft fhip
in the *Company's* fervice.—As this was
to be his laft voyage, and that which
would compleat his fortune, there
were many reafons to induce them to
defer their intended marriage till his
return, which would not exceed eigh-
teen, or twenty months, and which is
now in a few weeks expected.—

—I hope, fifter, fays CLERMONT,
turning round, that you will foon re-
leafe my friend, from the corner,
where you have penned him up—I
am got within fight of the *worm cakes*
and

and the *anodyne necklace*—but, however finish your story.—

—As this intended union, continued AMELIA, wore so fair a face to
those who most wished its completion,
though it disconcerted the secret
hopes which EDMUND still entertained
of getting part of his sister's fortune,
yet it precluded him from shewing
any disapprobation of it ;—he affected
to be greatly pleased,—and to the
few, who knew him as well as I did,
he even made himself ridiculous by
his over-acted satisfaction,—though all
this was put on but the better to conceal his designs, which were as ill
concerted, as they were base.

—There is evermore, Madam, said,
I, a strange degree of weakness, which
accompanies the actions of bad men ;
and

and it often feems, by this unguarded part of their conduct, that Providence makes them the inftruments of their own detection !—

Your remark, replied AMELIA, was fully juftified in EDMUND, who, fome time after Captain STERLING's departure, began to fpeak of him in cooler terms than he was wont; frequently throwing out in converfation with his fifter,—that the difpofitions of gentlemen trained to the fea, partook much of the unfteadinefs of the element they fail over ;—that they were in reality as little to be relied on, being fond of forming attachments in every port ;—and after thus gradually awakening her mind to diftruft, intimated, under the fanction of confidence, that he had reafon to believe there was one already fubfifting between

tween her admirer, and a Miss Danvers, whom the Captain had taken
out with him to Madrass;—that
however unpleasant the task was, his
own fraternal affection prompted him
to hint thus much; and to add, that
the constancy of his own sex could
not be much boasted of; and that the
woman who built her happiness on the
fidelity of a husband, knew not to
how slight a hold she trusted her
peace.——

This was probably just the point
his artifice led to,—his aim being
first to raise doubts of her lover, the
transition from which, to coolness,
would by no means be unnatural,—
and if her present engagement could
be diverted, it was possible, that dis-
appointment might make her cautious
of forming a second.—At all events,

it

it was a chance in his favour;—and I was much furprifed when fhe communicated to me what had paffed, to perceive that EDMUND had by his addrefs fo practifed on her mind, as to have greatly ftaggered her in her opinion of STERLING.—The fuppofed indignity difturbed her;—and the goodnefs of her own heart, left her too unguarded againft the duplicity of her brother.

I reprefented to MARIANNE, that the warmth of her affection muft have betrayed her into this ill-founded alarm, and made her inattentive to the channel through which it was communicated; — that as to Mifs DANVERS, I knew enough of her, totally to difcredit the illiberal fcandal, —that fhe had a firft coufin at MADRASS, who, having acquired a con-

fiderable

siderable fortune, had solicited her; and her mother (who were his nearest relations) to come over, and settle near him,—that the mother was ever esteemed a sensible, discreet lady,— and as this appeared to me, to be a most injurious aspersion, I assured her, that I would, for our mutual satisfaction, endeavour to trace it to its source.

—There being a ship on the point of sailing, which was destined immediately to MADRASS, there was a chance of its reaching that place nearly as soon as the INGOT; whose voyage thither, must have been retarded by her stay at the island of MADEIRA. —I wrote therefore, to Captain STERLING; and in the most delicate manner I could, told him the insinuations that had been poured into MARIANNE'S

ANNE's ears;—that the high opinion we both entertained of his honour, forbade us to give credit to them ;— but that I judged it proper to apprize him of the afperfion, that he might make my friend, who was the moft interefted about it, perfectly eafy.

My letter reached him at MA-DRASS; and fortunately came to hand juft as an exprefs was about fetting out, to come over-land to the *Company,* —by which he anfwered me in thofe ingenuous terms, which ever charac-terize innocence.—He told me, that the infinuations I alluded to, were fo unjuft, that he had forbore commu-nicating them to Mifs DANVERS, whom he had conducted in fafety to her coufin, who had made him the moft generous acknowledgments ;— that he doubted not but that this malicious artifice, originated from some one, who wished to sow dissention between him, and the object of his happiness;—in confirmation of which, he enclosed me a letter, under the signature of *A True Friend*, which had reached him just as he was sailing from MADEIRA,—reflecting on MARIANNE, as being fond of every new admirer; and counselling him not to preserve his heart for a woman, whose vanity sought for conquest over many.— But I have wrote, added he, to assure her, that my reliance on her affection, remains the same;—and that this work of some malevolent spirit, would, I trust, as little influence her's —as love can only live where confidence reigns; and it were impossible that confidence and jealousy could exist together.—

—Shocking

—Shocking as the idea was, MA-
RIANNE and myfelf, after duly weighing every circumftance, had now no
doubt, but that this intended mifchief
was the laft unhappy ftratagem of
EDMUND; nor did we long wait an
opportunity, to tax him as the author
of a defign, which ftruck at the peace
of fo many hearts.

—However the practice of well-
ftudied hypocrify may enable a man
to look a falfhood to the world, yet
events unprepared for, may, by their
fuddennefs, often furprife him into
conviction!—there is a language of
nature impreffed on the human countenance, far more powerful than words!
—and when I produced him the
anonymous letter fent to MADEIRA,
his features all bore witnefs againft a
tongue, that faltered in his own de-

fence—

fence;—he trembled—he changed colour,—the blood which before was
wont to animate his cheek, flew inftantly to his heart, and his heart
afhamed of it, dafhed it back into his
face.—His confufed juftification but
ftrengthened the proof—and he ftood
before us, a pitiable example to how
abject a fituation a man may degrade
himfelf, whofe mind is contaminated
by bafenefs, and difhonour.—

It was a fcene too painful to all, to
be prolonged; I therefore immediately clofed it, and leading MARIANNE
out of the room, told him, that as
he had fo effectually torn afunder
every tie of affection he might have
claimed in a fifter's heart, I now judged
it neceffary, not only for her happinefs, but for her fafety, that he fhould
have no future intercourfe with her;
—and

—and I was compelled to add, that as long as she regarded me as her protectress, my own roof would allow him none.—

Her fortune was soon after demanded and paid, through my solicitor, without any interview of the parties—and if a ship, that is gone out to INDIA, hath met with the INGOT at the CAPE, as it was expected she would, Captain STERLING, who was no stranger to some of the circumstances I have related, hath before this time been fully informed of all that hath passed since.—

—'Tis rarely now, that the name of EDMUND is mentioned; but I fear past events still sometimes come across her mind.—His conduct hath long extinguished the emotions of affection—yet her

her fenfibility makes her feel for his loft honour.——

——The picture, Madam, faid I, which you have drawn, prefents a character totally unworthy of dif-quieting the thoughts of your amiable friend—I wifh I could have fufficient influence to efface the recollection of it.——Her fentiments however, do cre-dit to her humanity—but it is in vain we are folicitous for the honour of thofe, who have not virtue enough themfelves to be the guardians of their own reputation !——

PLAIN

PLAIN TRUTH.

I HOLD it expedient for our happiness, says CLERMONT (throwing
the news-paper from his hand) that
we should fix our eyes, as we journey
forward, on such characters as spread
a sun-shine over human life, and not
on those dark ones that throw a gloom
over it.—We had better, I think,
sister, consign the hero of your story
to oblivion—or to the unenviable society of some of the *dramatis personæ*,
who have furnished paragraphs in the
paper I have been reading.—

" —*A married gentleman, with a*
" *large family, gone off to France with*
" *his young ward.*"—
—" *Two capital forgeries in the*
" *city.*"—

—" *Three*

—" *Three divorces litigating in Doc-*
" *tors Commons.*"—

—" *And an elderly lady of fashion*
" *found in bed with her postillion.*"—

Scandal enough in conscience for
one *Evening-post* !

—I would not willingly, continued
CLERMONT, believe the world to be
one jot less virtuous, than it was thirty
years ago,—but I am confident people
formerly took greater pains to conceal
their vices; and had at least the merit
of standing more in awe of public cen-
sure, which, by what I learn since
my return to ENGLAND, hath now far
less influence over their actions.—

Your observation, brother, replied
AMELIA, is but too just,—the indif-
ference shewn to it, and the countenance given to those, who have violated
the

the decorums of fociety, muft undoubtedly more forcibly ftrike you,
who have been fo many years abfent,
than it does us, who may have remarked the progrefs of this evil.—
The lady who helped the news-writer
to the laft paragraph, will not probably at her next rout, have one card-
table the lefs on the *poftillion's account*;
—nay, what will ftartle you more,—
thofe who cenfure her moft, will be of
her party ;—great dinners—great af-
femblies — or that happy innovation,
a Sunday-night's concert — though
given by people whofe conduct every
one condemns—will draw together
many, who one fhould think would
blufh to be feen at them;—and I much
fear, that the fafhionable careleffnefs
which is fhewn in matters of this nature, while it reflects but little credit

on

on the prefent age, may, by its example, be feverely felt in that which is to
fucceed it.——

Faith, Madam, refumed CLERMONT,
with fome warmth, in my opinion,
the countenancing thofe who are ca-
pable of ill actions, is but one remove from committing them;——fociety is equally infulted.——I cannot,
however, compliment you on the *re-
finement* of your manners, which feem
more calculated to take off *every* re-
ftraint, than to awaken *any* emulation ;
——the next generation will owe you
nothing for it.——If meritorious characters are, without difcrimination,
levelled with fuch, as have deviated
from the paths of honour, in God's
name *what becomes of virtue ?*——

——That, returned AMELIA, is but
too often left to be *its own reward,*——
and

and I truſt, it will never want argument to maintain its own conſequence, whilſt the *reward* it offers, is that *ſenſe of conſcious rectitude*, which the mind of man, however buoyed up by flattery and faſhion, can never long diſpenſe with the want of.——

——As it is much eaſier to find fault with the world, than to mend it, I put an end to the converſation, by ordering the backgammon table into the room ;——though I thought that my friend's ideas on the ſubject, were replete with *good ſenſe* and *plain truth.*

WHAT the deuce had I in my thoughts, when I popped my head into the ball-room ?—I, who have fo many things more effential to dance after, than a fiddle ?—But I hate to pafs a door, where every one is carrying their beft fpirits—befides, all the world was at MICHENER'S,—fo, paying my half crown, I took a fweat, on one of the fnug, fuperannuated benches.—

—Now of all the chapters I have ever wrote,—or ever fhall write,—either in the prefent,—or in any other work,— this, is that which muft be handled with the greateft nicety.—Some good angel guide my pen!—for a drop of ink too much, may blot out the intereft I

wifh

wifh to maintain in my reader's affection.—

—I am well aware, that this is the
chapter which will be the moft looked into,—be the moft thumbed,—
and after all, be that which will pleafe
the leaft, in the whole book.—Even
while I am this moment mufing over
it, my fancy anticipates the great demands that will be made for it, at the
circulating library.—I hear Mr. HALL,
in the moft obliging manner, affert,
that *it is out.*—" But it is the *fecond
volume* I am *dying* for,—and my coufin Peggy will be quite *diftraĉted*, if fhe
cannot have it this evening."—

If you will believe me, Madam, re-
turns Mr. HALL (with the moft feeling concern for the fad events of *Death*
and *Diftraĉtion* prediĉted to arife from
this

this difappointment) I have no lefs than fix fets, and not one of either of the volumes at home.—Lady FANNY in the ROPE-WALK, has been down twice herfelf after the *fecond*,—and two ladies on the PARADE, are, I fear, affronted at fending fo often, without obtaining it :—In the mean time, Madam, I have the TOYSHOP at your fervice, or I can fend you home now, THE DELICATE EMBARRASS-MENT.—

—I wifh from my heart, that this eager curiofity after the prefent chapter, be not fomewhat ftimulated by a little tincture, compounded of a fmall portion of felf-fufficiency, and ill-nature,—which, however unwilling we are to own it, I fear moft of us carry about; and which prompts us but

but too often, to divert ourfelves at another's expence.——

——I am confident, that many will expect to fee here a collection of portraits drawn from real life—to find fome awkward minuet recorded,—or fome miftaken graces they may themfelves have recollected, and condemned.—But whoever thou art, who turneft over this page, if fuch be thy expectations, thou knoweft but little of his difpofition who now is writing it.—My pen may ftigmatize vice and folly ;—it may blame *the facrifice*—but never fhall mark *the votary.*——

——Was not I ingenuous enough to tell you beforehand, that this chapter would prove but an unfatisfactory one ?—It could not be otherwife.—The fubject was in truth totally out of my way.——

9   —Be

—Be fo good Madam, as to read
the title of my book—

S K E T C H E S

FROM

N A T U R E.

—Who could ever dream of making
any in a ball-room?—

—And fo my dear creatures you
may all dance on, juft as you did before.—

THE BALL-ROOM.

HAVING, in the laſt page, made a genteel bow to all maiden aunts,—goſſipping dowagers,—and to the unneceſſarily inquiſitive of both ſexes,—I will, with my reader's indulgence, offer an obſervation or two, that has frequently occurred to me in a ball-room.

—I am fond of every amuſement that brings people together in cheerfulneſs and good-humour.—Dancing is unqueſtionably one of the number; —it is enlivening, though from different motives, both to youth, and age;—it gives a certain air and deportment to the perſon who is well grounded in the art; and ſets off the young, and the elegant, with great

advantage to each other.—I was myfelf once a pupil of the famous MAR-
CEL at PARIS, though no one who
now views my curved and ungain figure, would fuppofe it.—My fpirits
however, are to this moment always
in the dance;—and my long legs have
ftill fuch a propenfity to be moved
by the found of a fiddle, that in the
corner where I was ftationed laft
night, they would willingly have
kept pace with the tune, had not I
perceived that my knees were beat-
ing time, againft a certain part of a
very fat lady before me, which lapped
fix inches over them, and which (had
there been a poffibility) I fhould
have truly rejoiced fhe had left at
home.—

—I wifh, by the bye, that in theatres, and other places of public re-
fort,

fort, where the proprietors are interefted to place the benches, much
clofer together than fuits the eafe of
the fpectator, *a mafter of the ceremo-
nies* was appointed; who, as people
feated themfelves, fhould take their
altitudes, projections, and circum-
ferences, and difpofe them in fuch a
manner, that they might have nothing to complain of, before, or behind.—

—But to return to the dance.—

I muft own I am rather forry to obferve, that the COTILLON begins to be
introduced into our balls.—How far
more experience in thofe dances, may
improve us in them, I know not;
but I have fcarcely as yet, feen the
figure gone through without inter-
ruption.—Befides, we feem to want

that

that feſtivity, and that *enjoûémenf,* which hath made me view them with ſo much pleaſure in FRANCE.—Whoever has attended to them, even in the BOIS DE BOULOGNE, *au* SAINT ESPRIT, or at any of the *guinguettes* about PARIS, muſt have remarked, that *the ſoul* dances *with the body,* and every feature of the face tells you it does.——

Another objection to their coming into public uſe here, is, that they occupy a very large ſpace in a room, and employ but very few; ſo that in a crowded aſſembly, the far greater number muſt be merely ſpectators, and the few who dance, become extremely diſtinguiſhed;—whilſt the whimſical ſteps, and high capers, which are practiſed in our

5   ENGLISH

ENGLISH COTILLON, furnish more of a *spectacle*, than many ladies may choose to contribute to.——

——Our own COUNTRY DANCES, have the peculiar advantage of admitting a very large number to join in them.—— I have seen them practised and admired, in most parts of EUROPE ; and they are in my idea, infinitely better calculated to display, that elegant ease of motion, which has been so properly termed *swimming in the dance* ; and which would inevitably be lost, should we apply to them, the theatrical steps, which the professors of the COTILLON now teach.

——As dancing is an act of hilarity, I think in general, that we appear to make too *serious* a business of it.——The exercise gives an impulse to circulation.——We may also allow

some-fomething to the animation of mufic, —and far more to the animation of fentiment, naturally excited by being engaged in fo pleafing a familiarity, with the fex we moft wifh to appear favourably to;—and yet, in almoft every ball-room, how many couple do we fee *journeying* down a dance, with fuch *ferious* countenances, as if they were rather toiling through a pennance impofed them, than engaged in a voluntary amufement!—

—It is certainly being undefirably philofophical, to feel pleafure, without expreffing it.—

—Nothing is more calculated than the MINUET, to fhew an elegant figure to advantage;—it is the art of moving with grace and eafe,—but to dance in that degree of tafte, as to command admiration, requires early inftruction,

inftruction, good judgment, and a nice ear, fuperadded to many perfo-nal endowments.—As greatly to excel therefore, in this accomplifhment, can happen but to few, a moderate knowledge of it may be difpenfed with, and attended to ;—but it were far better declined by the many, who attempt it, without any of the re-quifites.

—Acts, which are the *efforts of grace*, ought to be *gracefully* per-formed !—And as there is fome path, or other, in which every one may walk with propriety and fuccefs, it is a fad miftake, when we place our-felves, unneceffarily, in fuch con-fpicuous fituations, as we are totally unfuited to appear in.—

When difcord agitated the affembly

of

of· the Gods, and their wrangles
had made a bear-garden of OLYM-
PUS, HOMER makes VULCAN take up
the goblet of Nectar, and hand it
about among them, that they might
drink themfelves into better humour.

. —Now VULCAN was altogether one
of the beft of the whole crew;—he
was honeft,—he was induftrious,—he
was a peace-maker,—and added to
all—he was a hufband for any age,
or any country;—for he could amufe
himfelf with forging a nail, or a
horfe-fhoe, while his wife was cuckold-
ing him in heaven, and on earth.—

—It was an abfurdity in VULCAN,
who was naturally very awkward,—
and accidentally very lame,—to af-
fect an office which demanded the
grace

grace of a GANYMEDE;—the confequence was,—that he diverted the attention of every deity prefent, from
their own concerns, and forced a good-
humoured laugh from the whole affembly.—

THE

LA Pierre hath so much vivacity, blended with so much natural courtesy,—and possesses besides, so strong a disposition to thrust himself into every place where intelligence is to be procured, that nothing is stirring from one end of Margate to the other, that doth not come to his knowledge.—He is never without a *bouquet* in his bosom, which he presents to the first *fille de chambre* of his acquaintance that he meets ;—his great pride is to be admitted to their tea-tables; and his easy, happy spirits, make him perfectly at home, wherever he goes.—

—The poor fellow could hardly make my coffee at breakfast, with-

I   out

out burning his fingers, from his impatience to tell me, that he had been down on the *Pier* to fee two INDIA-MEN, which were lying off the town, and had come to an anchor the preceding evening,—pulling, at the fame time, from his jacket-pocket, a fqueezed-up filk handkerchief, to fhew me, which he had bought from fome one who had been aboard.

—Pray have you inquired, faid I, whether - - -

O oui, Monfieur, vous voulez dire - - -

What would you anfwer my queftion before you know it?—

—No, Sir; but I fuppofed you was going to afk, if either of thefe was the INGOT—fo I ran down to the circulating library, to get their names, —and *Monfieur* HALL tells me, that the INGOT is expected to be in the

DOWNS

DOWNS in lefs than three weeks,—
being failed for IRELAND, to do her
bufinefs there,—or the Captain's bufinefs, — or fomebody's bufinefs, —
apparemment pour faire fes affaires.

—If *Monfieur* fhould not ride out
this morning, there are two or three
fervants, who live with the FRENCH
family in the ROPE-WALK, who
have got leave to go aboard, and
would take me with them in their
boat.—I never was in a large fhip;
and befides, I fhould like to buy two
or three fans to give to Madam
AMELIA's maids, who are always fo
polite to me.—

—Thou art heartily welcome to
make one of the party, faid I, and
take thy own time.—I fee, LA PIERRE,
thou wilt never be worth a piece of
Trente fous, while there is a bawble to
be

be purchafed, or a petticoat to prefent it to.—After this permiffion, he
would not have ftayed to get his
breakfaft, though he had been fure
of eating nothing for the next twenty-
four hours.

—No circumftance makes the towns
on the coaft of KENT more alive, than
the coming in of the INDIA-MEN—all
is then in motion.—I took a walk on
the cliffs on purpofe to enjoy the
buftle of the fcene;—the fea looked
uncommonly gay,—the fhips riding
at anchor, with their colours flying,
—boats bufied in carrying them frefh
provifions from the fhore,—fo many
little veffels plying about them, and
thofe of the cuftom-houfe, lying befide them, as guards,—while parties
of company from MARGATE, and
others, who come down from LONDON

to meet their friends on board, covered the fine blue furface with a
multitude of little fails.—

—A fhip that hath traverfed the
globe, and cut her paffage through a
world of waters, that, after fuftaining
a variety of climates, and all the
conflicts of oppofing elements, ar-
rives at laft at her deftined port, hath
ever appeared to me as an object
which conveys an infinite pleafure to
the mind!—I cannot but reflect, that
every Being fhe brings back, ftanding in one, or other of the relations
of hufband, parent, fon, or friend,—
hath many hearts that anxioufly beat
for his return,—many eyes that wait
with eagernefs to catch the firft look,
—and ears that impatiently long to
know, how the faid interval of abfence hath paffed away!—When the
imagination

imagination multiplies this, by the number that forms the complement of a large ship, it views all the tendereft affections of the foul, fet afloat by her fafe arrival !—

— Whilft benevolence contemplates fuch a vifionary fcene, the viciffitudes of life induce our humanity to offer up a filent wifh,—that no tale of woe may remain to be unfolded, whofe diftrefs fhall overcloud the fun-fhine, or blaft the happy expectations that hope hath cherifhed !—

THE

THE FORT.

I KNOW not how it hath come about, that I have led my reader through one volume, and half through a ſecond, without ever once conduct-ing him up to the FORT;—where, if he is a lover of NATURE, he will be charmed,—and if he is not, I fear I ſhall have but little intereſt with him, either on the FORT, or elſe-where—who have vowed myſelf to her ſervice, and devoted all my attention to this glorious miſtreſs.—It is from a ſhabby bench, placed on this ſum-mit, that I frequently muſe over the noble proſpect that is ſpread beneath. —Before me, the eye is loſt in ſea and air,—but extending ſideways, takes in the winding cliffs from the NORTH

FORELAND

FORELAND to the Ifle of SHEPEY, with
all the interfperfed villages to the
left, that enrich the coaft,—termi-
nated by the church of the Two
SISTERS—whofe double fpires not only
embellifh the fcene, but rife up a
faithful guide to the mariner.

—As I returned along the northern
cliff from my walk, intending to
make my accuftomed halt at the FORT,
I perceived my bench was poffeffed
by a lady; and whom I found, on a
nearer approach, to be the amiable
MARIANNE.—I knew fhe could not
but be an interefted fpectator of the
fcene before her; which muft, in idea,
anticipate the return of one, on whom
her future. happinefs fo much depended.—She was dreffed fimply elegant; and wore, in compliment to
her Lover who had prefented her with

it, a beautiful chintz negligee, tied
up with green ribband, and a hat decorated with ribband of the fame colour.—As I fat down by her, fhe affumed a fmile, though there was a pen-
fivenefs on her brow; yet at the fame
time, there appeared fo much fenfe and
character in her countenance, as could
not but intereft whoever approached
her.—I complimented her on the arrival of the fhips, that were then lying full in our view, and on the welcome news they had brought, of the
INGOT's being fo near home.—I meet
it indeed, fhe replied, as a circumftance of real joy ;—nor ought I to
figh, if the path of life I have trod-
den, hath been uneven, provided it
leads to happinefs at laft.—

—And what better termination,
faid I, can the fmootheft conduct us
to ?—

to ?—It is no unpleasing idea, which some have entertained, that every one hath a *guardian spirit* hovering near, whose friendly office it is, to give us safe convoy through all the difficulties which lie acrofs our way, and to support us under the severeft trials. —Why may we not conceive this imaginary exiftence to be HOPE ?— We cannot, I am fure, truft to a fafer guide, nor wifh, in the hours of adverfe fortune, to be led forward by the hand of a more cheering companion.—

But prithee, my gentle lady, what thorn hath been rankling in thy poor little bofom ?—Thou haft hit, perhaps, upon fome melancholy page of life, and turned down the leaf to ruminate on it.—Who meets not with it ?—It is for the perufal of all the

fons

fons and daughters of man;—nor is
it in the end, unprofitable reading,
—fince.it fhews ambition its vanity,
— pride its meannefs, — wealth its
emptinefs,—and learning its infuffi-
ciency;—and, by levelling all ranks
of mortals, annihilates the paltry
diftinctions of the world!—

O Sir! returned MARIANNE (fetch-
ing a figh) O Sir, I have a brother! - - -

. —Who is, replied I, unworthy
your regard.—

—One, whofe difpofition - - -

—Was never allied to your virtues.—

—There only remains for me - - -

—To wipe him from your memory,
and leave him to the bittereft of all
reproaches—his own—.

. —I dare believe I am an echo to
your thoughts;—but my dear, good
girl,

girl, AMELIA hath opened to me your whole fituation, and the painful trials your fenfibility hath fuftained.—I have a tear to give every child of forrow;—and I truft, the fountain which fupplies it, will never be dry!—But I would now rather perfonate your *guardian fpirit*; and, turning our backs on difficulties furmounted, look forward with you, to objects that wear a happier face.— It is not a few bad characters we may chance to meet with, that fhould put us out of humour with the world.— It is for our peace, to recollect, that the GREAT DIRECTOR of this immenfe work of creation, is continually raifing up others, who have breafts that glow with virtuous fentiments, where congenial hearts may fecurely repofe.—

Believe

Believe me, MARIANNE, 'it hath only been by viewing events on the favourable fide, that I have myfelf bore fo well the buffets of fortune. —For I have alfo, among my family pictures, fome abominable originals, —and fuch terrible, ftrong likeneffes too, that out of humanity, I keep a curtain over them.—

—I verily think, in the difpofition I then was, that to divert her ideas, I fhould have pulled it a little afide, to have given her a peep at one, or two of them,—had we not been interrupted by three or four ladies of our acquaintance, who were come up with their glaffes in their hands, to take a view of the new-arrived INDIA-MEN, and immediately joined us at our bench.—I believe MARIANNE wifhed them, juft at this

this time, any where elfe ;—but they faved me the pain of uncovering a fingle portrait, and fully anfwered the fame purpofe :—For among the many advantages that attend perfect good-breeding, there is one, that hath never been enumerated, though far from being the leaft ;—and that is, the relief which the mind, when under any depreffion, receives, upon the fudden intrufion of company, by finding itfelf compelled to beftow on another, that attention, which would otherwife be rivetted to its own fituation.—

THE

DIDO, foundrefs and queen of CARTHAGE, is the firft woman of antiquity, who is recorded for *driving a good bargain.*—The JEWS and MONEY-JOBBERS, have the higheft veneration for her memory;—and I am informed, that *fhe*, and her *bull's hide*, is a favourite toaft among all thofe people,—not only within the purlieus of DUKE's PLACE, but in the neighbourhood of every *fynagogue* in EUROPE.—

—There are two ways of meafuring any thing, as the widow of SICHÆUS well knew; and as every fhop-keeper, who retails commodities, perfectly underftands,—and the poffeffor of this knowledge, muft ever

have

have the balance of trade in his favour.——

—Whoever is to open a confiderable
commerce with the world, it will be
much more worth to him, than the
whole round of fciences, not only to
know to an inch, his own meafure,
and how far he could on a pinch
ftretch it,—but alfo to be fully acquainted with the meafure his neigh-
bour goes by;—for, by thus fkil-
fully calculating the longitude,—lati-
tude,—altitude,—and rectitude, of the
parties he has to deal with, he will be
enabled equally to guard againft the
fallacy of a minifter, or the impofi-
tion of his taylor.——

With refpect to the world, La
Pierre was a mere infant,—ever
pleafed with its coral, and its bells,
—but without a tooth to injure any
one !——

one !—The fimplicity of his character,
made him daily meet with fome fan-
cied diftrefs, which, to another, who
was more hackneyed in the ways
of mankind, would only have paffed
among the common occurrences of
life ;—though, to fay truth, nothing
fat long on his mind ; a deep figh
or two blew off the load, and a
whiftle, or a fong, which foon followed, obliterated every trace of its
weight.—It chanced, however, that I
got to my lodgings foon after his return from the INDIA-MAN, and before
either the figh, or the tune was come
to his aid, or had effaced the firft
impreffion of his prefent grievance ;
which was fufficiently apparent in LA
PIERRE's countenance, that was at all
times an index to his bofom, and
like a well-printed fhop-bill, notified
every

every concern his heart had to dif-
pofe of.—The morning which had
promifed fo much fatisfaction, had
been over-clouded with circumftances,
both unlooked for, and unpleafant.
—As the poor fellow's pride was to
be as fmart as poffible, whenever any
females were to be of his party; in
gallanting one of them into the
boat, at the Parade ftairs, he unfortunately flipt almoft up to his knees in
the muddy water, and quite disfi-
gured his white filk ftockings.—
This was an event which might have
difconcerted a better FRENCH philo-
fopher than LA PIERRE, and was but
a prologue to worfe difafters ;—for a
frefh breeze fpringing up, when they
had got about a mile from the fhore,
the tofling of the waves fo difturbed
his empty ftomach, as to make him
wretchedly

wretchedly fick, till he got aboard the INDIA-MAN;—the civility of every one there, made him foon forget what he had fuffered;—he purchafed the little trifles he wifhed;—and would have returned to fhore perfectly fick, and happy again, had not fome cuf-tom-houfe officers hailed the boat, and ftripped from him, and his party, the poor fix-penny cargoes they had been fo far to fetch;—nor was this all—for they took away befides the new INDIA *filk handkerchief* he had bought in the morning, and which, in his hurry to fet off, he had forgot to put out of his pocket.—

Quels miferables! cries LA PIERRE —*quels barbares!*—

—That, fays I,—and fending them to the devil in good FRENCH, is all you have for it:—

—Why

—Why, what do you think Sir, added he, the king can get by his duty on a couple of INDIA Fans, that his people are fo watchful for his intereft?

That is a queftion, returned I, that might have puzzled the calculations of your countryman, DE MOIVRE,— but confidering the number of hands it rubs againft, before it reaches the *Exchequer*, I fhould conceive his net profit could not exceed the four hundredth and feventy-third part of one of your *liards*.—I am an avowed enemy to all counterband dealings,— as well as to all the little dirty infolence of office — but if you had not been a novice in thefe matters, you might have obtained an eafier folution to your queftion, by offering a

restitution

reſtitution fee, and ſo purchaſing your fans a ſecond time.——

Mon Dieu! exclaims LA PIERRE, what offer *a bribe*, Sir, to a king's ſervant?——

Ah! pour cela, oui, or to a king's miſtreſs,——or to a king's any thing—only give it a different name.——Modern language hath made it *palatable* to all ranks, under the idea of *acknowledgment*, or *attention*;——as the diſguſtful ingredients of an apothecary's vial, are ſwallowed without reluctance, when the label denotes it to be a *cordial mixture.*——

Now as this *cordial mixture* muſt, like all other cordials, be adminiſtered for various purpoſes,——as alſo to various conſtitutions, —— and be ſo tempered, as to act either as a *ſtimulator,*

lator, or *soporific*, as occasion may require,—it is expedient, that it be always judiciously applied; and, when
well adapted to the stomach that is
to receive it, can very rarely fail of
insuring success.—

—No one better understood how to
manage *a bribe* artfully, or to tamper
with the passions, than the *Abbè*
FRONTIN. — He was, perhaps, too
much addicted to pleasure, and intrigue,
but had much wit, and infinite good
humour;—he possessed a presence of
mind, equal to any emergency; and
was so happy in his address, as to be
almost irresistible.—

—By the by, I have never gone
into the church of SAINT SULPICE at
PARIS, without lamenting, that he
should lie there without having even
a stone of two feet square to record

7   his

his memory, who had talents so superior to the herd of *Abbès*, who litter the BOULEVARDS and the THUILLERIES, and have nothing but their black cloaks to distinguish them.——

——*Madame de* CHATEAUROUGE was arrived at that period of life, when ladies in FRANCE turn *dévotes*, and confine all their favours within the pale of the church.——SAINTE THERESE observes, in some of her visionary compositions, that women must occasionally *transplant* their affections ;—— and thus it is, that FRENCH *saints* usually take the leavings of FRENCH *sinners*.——

This lady had taken a pretty long time to settle her conscience ;——and there remained some points of reform yet unadjusted, when she called in to her assistance the *Abbè* FRONTIN, who

who very foon became her intimate
attendant, accompanied her frequently to mafs, was conftantly of all her
parties, read to her in her clofet, and
aired with her in the Bois de Boulogne.

It chanced one fummer's afternoon, that *Madame de* Chateaurouge, after her coffee, had retired
into an apartment which looked into
the garden, to enjoy the frefh air,
and the fragrance of a little orangery,
that was ranged in a femicircle before the windows, which were thrown
open.—As the fun ftill fhot obliquely
into the room, the green luftring
curtains were dropped, to give a
more pleafing tone of light.—The
Abbè was feated by her on a fopha;
and, at her requeft, was entertaining her with a new piece of Crebil-

LON, called *Les egarements du Cœur et de l'Esprit,* which had juſt then appeared, and had much excited the curioſity of the public.——

——I leave it to thoſe who are fond of inveſtigating cauſes and effects, to find out how it came to paſs that *Madame de* CHATEAUROUGE, as the *Abbè* proceeded in the work, with emphaſis, and ſpirit, had infenſibly reclined her head on his ſhoulder, whilſt the *Abbè,* holding the book in his right hand, had inadvertently dropped his left arm, acroſs her lap. ——The cenforious, may miſinterpret the poſition they ſat in——the candid, attribute it to accident, or the weather——and people of a ſentimental turn, may aſcribe it merely to the having their attention abſorbed in the novel, and to the ingenuity of the

writer

writer in thus interesting the paffions.—It is my province only to fay
the fact was as related; and a little
guft of air on a fudden fwelling the
curtains, the leads on its ceffation
falling againft the wainfcot, gave
three or four repeated raps,—which
being heard by GRISON, the old *maître
d'Hôtel*, who was fettling the houfe-
book in the next room, and who,
miftaking thefe raps for a method,
which his lady (who was a little lame
and unwieldy) fometimes ufed, to
fummon him with her crutched ftick,
when fhe fat at a diftance from the
bell, gently opened the door, and conceiving immediately, by one glance,
that he could not be wanted,—inftantly fhut it again as gently,—and
fat himfelf down very compofedly,
to his accqunts,—for he had lived
H 2   long

long enough in the family to have
the fagacity of knowing, when he
ought to fee,—and when not.—

The *Abbè*, who had juft caught a
glimpfe of the *maître d'hôtel* as he
peeped in, thought it advifeable to
fecure his intereft;—and as foon as
the ftory was at a full ftop, laid down
his book, and walked into the adjoining room where GRISON was,—
who hearing fomebody ftep towards
the door, threw himfelf againft the
back of the chair, and reclining his
head on his hand, with his elbow on
the table, pretended to be found
afleep.

The *Abbè*, who, as I hinted before, was never on any occafion in
the fmalleft degree embarraffed, knew,
by appearances, that he was fure of
his man; and gently laying a *Louis d'or*

on

on each of his eyelids, faid, with a tone of pleafantry, "there are none "who fee fo little as thofe whofe eyes "are *well clofed*."—

—"True, Sir," replied GRISON,— "and if you will flip another be- "tween my lips, you will be certain "to make me *dumb*, as well as "*blind*."—

—This fellow would have made an admirable Revenue officer,—

—In any place where *no duty* was expected.

NATURE.

WHOEVER hath paſſed any length of time at theſe places of public reſort, by the ſea-ſide, muſt have remarked that there is conſtantly a flux and reflux of the company who frequent them; and that the ſhores have their revolutions and changes, as well as the element that flows along their ſides.—I often, as I pace up and down the PARADE, miſs faces I have been accuſtomed to meet in my daily walks, and am ſtared at by others that are totally new to me—nor is it a ſmall pleaſure to me, who am looking after NATURE at every ſtep, to obſerve features tinged with the hue of returning health, which a few weeks before I had ſeen overcaſt

with

with languor; and limbs beginning to move with freedom, which were lately contracted by pain and dis- ease.—

As I have before convinced my readers of the benefit of *smelling the sea-mud*, so these occurrences con- vince me of the benefit of using sea- water.—As an added proof of its effi- cacy, I popped yesterday on the *fat lady* in the *Brunswick*, whom I before mentioned as being so lame, and un- wieldy, and whom I had given over as incurable, when she was helped down the side of the Hoy.—I was perfectly amazed to see the briskness of her air, and her round, laughing countenance, half buried in a FRENCH night-cap;—and though she still re- tains a considerable hitch in her gait; yet she walked with no other aid than

H 4   a lady's

a lady's arm, on which she reclined, and one of Mr. HALL's *pastoral twined crooks*, which no female of any taste can appear without.——Even my own lean carcase, though I neither intentionally *smell the mud*, nor ever come in contact with the water, is both strengthened and plumped up by the sea-air,——and my weak constitution, which has, for two volumes, been so great a plague to the reader, and for many a year, a far greater one, to me, is from the same cause so much strengthened, that I have but even now, with eighty or ninety long strides, mounted up to the FORT, without a single halt to fetch breath.——

——How sweet is thy return, O HEALTH! thou rosy cherub!——my soul leaps forward to meet thee, whose true value thy absence can only teach us!——

us!—When thou comeſt, *with heal-ing on thy wings*; when every part, and nerve, and artery, are obedient to their office; and when this compli-cated machine is ſo perfectly har-monized, that we perceive not that we have any part, or nerve, or artery, belonging to us, how ſweetly is the mind then attuned to receive pleaſure from every inlet of ſenſe?

—GOD of my life! who numbereſt my days, teach me to meet with gratitude, or patience, the good, or ill, which the tide of time ſhall float down with them!—but never with-draw from me thoſe native ſpirits, which have been the cheering com-panions of my exiſtence, and have ſpread a gilding upon every thing around me!—that I may continue to view, with rapture, the inexhauſtible

volume

volume of NATURE that is thrown open before me ; on every page of which is charactered the impreſſion of thy OMNIPOTENT HAND !—

As I often indulge a meditating diſpoſition on the old bench upon the FORT, where I am now ſeated, it is matter of amuſement to conſider the immenſe variety, that a ſhort ſpace of time produces in the ſame natural objects;—every change of light,— every alteration in the atmoſphere, gives them a different appearance.— I have juſt been contemplating the wide ſcene of waters before me; that hath lately been darkened by ſome clouds which overhung it.—I ſee it emerging into new day.—I perceive its green hue warming into purple tints:—as I direct my eye as far as it can ſtretch, I view the ſun, from be-

hind

hind a veil that conceals it, ſhooting down its rays on a limited circum-ference, and brightening all the edges of the waves.—And now its broad orb appears in full glow; deſcending almoſt level with the ſea—the whole weſtern canopy is illumi-nated.—It trembles a little while on the extremity of the horizon, and at laſt plunges from the ſight.

—Thoſe who may be diſpoſed to contraſt the works of NATURE, with the moſt boaſted labours of ART, will find the firſt, ever new and permanent, while the latter, the inſtant they have attained their *limited perfection*, ap-proach toward a ſlow, but a ſure de-cline.—

The pride of a potent monarch, may be gratified, in erecting ſome magnificent temple to his god;—he

may

may perpetuate the remembrance of his anceftors, by fuperb maufoleums;—he may command the daring pyramid to fhoot upward to the fkies,—may infcribe his victories on the trophied column,—or regifter his triumphs on the fculptured arch!—He may call an ADAM to execute his great defigns;—who, while he is fulfilling the wifhes of his fovereign, may himfelf deliver down to a feries of generations unborn, the noblett records of his own genius, and tafte. — But even though no accident fhould abridge their duration,—yet the revolving feafons foon fully their beauty;—and the filent power of Time gradually fhakes their foundations; and at laft levels them with the duft.—While thy works, O NATURE, remain uninjured; — ever

changing,

changing, and ever reviving, thou shineft unconfcious of decay!—ftill bright in immortal youth!—

And yet more lovely far doft Thou appear, when Thou commandeft our attention in thy *active fcenes,* and beameft from the mind with all thofe irradiations of VIRTUE, HONOUR, and BENEVOLENCE, which dignify humanity.—Thefe may be deemed the *fun-fhine* of the *moral world!* —that warms,—that brings forward, —and ripens the foul to perfection! —And if fometimes, in contemplating the pictures of real life, one fees with pain the canvafs darkened with worthlefs characters, they fhould be viewed but as deep fhades, which, however they may interrupt thy native brightnefs, yet by their contraft

5

more

more forcibly imprefs the amiablenefs of thy luftre !—

Full of fuch fentiments, I frequently, from this cliff, caft a look toward
RECULVER, and drop a figh, to the
memory of thofe beloved SISTERS,
who were in their lives fo undivided,
and whofe unfhaken union hath there
been fo long recorded.—

Confidering how many furveys
have been publifhed of this county,
and how much the zeal for antiquity hath for many years prevailed
amongft us; it is fomewhat fingular,
that fo flight mention fhould have
been made of this extraordinary
building; of which little more hath
been faid, than that *the church was
formerly confiderable, having ftill two
goodly fpiring fteeples.*

As

As people in general only speak of this edifice merely as being accidentally an advantageous *sea-mark*, unknowing of the cause by which it became so;—I am happy that it is in my power, in this remote period of time, to gratify the curiosity of those, who hereafter may visit these shores.——

I have long wished, my dear JEN-NY, to relate to thee this interesting story.—To Thee, whose heart NA-TURE hath so sweetly harmonized, that it vibrates at the slightest touch of another's sorrow; and is therefore worthy to hear a tale of distress.——

Several years ago, being on a journey to SPA, I was detained some time in the university of LOUVAIN, by an accidental illness, which seized me

me on the road.—During my ſtay, I
made an acquaintance with an IRISH
jeſuit, who honoured me with many
civilities, and whom I found a very
intelligent companion.—He ſhewed
me whatever he thought moſt curious
in the place; though, except the great
library, and the public ſchools, there
is but little worth notice.

I was however much pleaſed with
two manuſcript volumes, which I
met with in the library of one of the
colleges; — they chiefly contained
anecdotes relative to ſome ENGLISH
families, and to ſeveral hiſtorical,
and monaſtical antiquities; and were
the memorials of a DOMINICAN Friar
of CANTERBURY, who quitted ENG-
LAND at the time of the *Reformation*,
and retired to LOUVAIN; — at his
death he bequeathed them, together
with

with other curious books, to the college where they then were.—My friend, who was one of its members, procured the manufcript to be lent me ;—and, in turning over many fubjects far lefs interefting, I met with the hiftorical account of this church. —I have divefted it of the obfolete language of the times, but the fubftance of it is nearly as follows.—

THE STORY OF THE TWO SISTERS.

TOWARDS the end of thofe troublefome times, when ENG-LAND was fhook by the feuds of the houfes of YORK and LANCASTER, there refided, in a village near the banks of the MEDWAY, a gentleman, whofe name was GEOFFRY DE SAINT CLAIR, defcended from a family of great antiquity, and repute in thofe parts.—— The many launces, and pieces of armour, that hung round the old hall, did not render it more refpectable, than did the unbounded benevolence of its prefent poffeffor.——The poor fat at his gate, and bleffed his liberal hand; and never a pilgrim repofed in his porch, without remembering, in his orifons, its hofpitable owner.

SAINT

Saint Clair had allied himſelf in
marriage with the Lady Margaret
de Boys, a woman of high birth, and
rare endowments; whoſe accompliſhments might have embelliſhed the
greateſt ſcenes, had not a love of domeſtic life, and a religious caſt of
mind, induced her to prefer retirement.—All her leiſure hours, which
her family did not call for, were ſpent
in duties, which, in that age, ladies
of the nobleſt rank exerciſed, without
thinking they demeaned their ſta-
tions;—ſhe relieved the indigent,—
adviſed with the unfortunate,—viſited
the ſick,—and brought up her *Twin
Daughters*, Frances and Isabella,
in the ſame ſentiments;—accuſtoming
them very early, to attend upon her
in all thoſe acts of primitive piety.—
As theſe young ladies were the ſole

I 2   iſſue

issue of SAINT CLAIR and Lady MAR-
GARET, they devoted their whole attention to their education; and had
the comfort to find in their minds, so
rich a soil, that every thing prospered
which was planted in them:—no
useful knowledge was omitted,—no
external accomplishment neglected.—

FRANCES and ISABELLA were now
arrived at the age of twenty-five.—
The amiableness of their characters,
their enlarged understandings, and
the gracefulness of their persons, won
the admiration and esteem of all who
approached them.—They had, from
similitude of manners, and sentiment,
contracted such a rare affection for
each other, that it seemed as if NA-
TURE, by forming them together in
the womb, had prepared them for
that extraordinary union, which was

3 . to

to diftinguifh their lives,—and for thofe effufions of elevated friendfhip, which the lofs of their exemplary mother was one day to call forth. —Nor was this event very remote; Lady MARGARET was feized by a fudden illnefs, which, in a few days, carried her off, and defolated one of the happieft families in the world.—

It would be difficult to defcribe the founds of woe, which, on this occafion, echoed through all the manfion, or the fighs of the difconfolate poor, under the windows.— The grief of SAINT CLAIR, after the many years of uninterrupted happinefs that he had enjoyed with Lady MARGARET, in its firft attack, almoft overpowered his reafon; — FRANCES and ISABELLA had the weight of a father's forrow added to their own;

which

which compelled them to smother
their feelings, great as they were,
and to assume a fortitude their hearts
disavowed. —

   —Lovely mourners! — more lovely
in your tears! — Methinks I see you now,
bathed in filial sorrow, — standing by,
and supporting your distracted parent
— striving in vain to tear him from
the coffin, which he will not suffer his
servants to close, — still demanding,
in wild utterance, again, and again —
one last — last look ! —

   —Heavens!—how severe a distress!
—If any reader hath been in a situation, to ask for *a last look* of what
is most dear to him,—and what he is
going to be deprived of for ever—
he alone can best judge, how much
that bosom is agonized, that urges the
request !—

                Though

Though Saint Clair called in aid all his philofophy, to fupport himfelf under the lofs of his beloved Lady Margaret, yet he was worn, by a filent forrow, which had fo vifible an effect on his health, as to menace his life; and which, in about a year, put an end to it.—

In this mournful interval, the greateft comfort his dejected daughters received, was, from the frequent vifits of their uncle, John de Saint Clair—who was at that time, Abbot of the monaftery of Saint Augustin, in Canterbury; of which place, there are, at this day, fuch noble remains exifting.—He was the younger brother of Geoffry, though there was but the difference of a year between them; and was reputed to be a man of fo much learning and virtue, that Saint

Clair,

CLAIR, by his will, recommended his children to his care and protection; bequeathing to each of them, a very large inheritance.*—

—The

* The ingenious Mr. BATTELY, in his addition to SOMNER, has given us a succession of the ABBOTS of SAINT AUGUSTIN, from the year 598, down to the Reformation; extracted chiefly from THORN, who was himself a Monk of that foundation.—But THORN's Chronicle coming no lower than 1419, the names of the ABBOTS from that period, are collected, as Mr. BATTELY tells us, from a manuscript relating to the monastery, and are given without dates.

We do not find the name of JOHN DE SAINT CLAIR in the list; but about the time alluded to, in the LOUVAIN *Manuscript*, mention is made of JOHN THE ABBOT, without the addition of his family name; and so doubtful is it, who this JOHN was, that some had supposed it to be JOHN DUNSTER, PRIOR.

—The manner in which FRANCES had been brought up, added to her natural turn of mind, and the example of a mother fhe fo much revered, determined her to a life of religious retirement;—and a great convent of BENEDICTINE NUNS, not very diftant from FEVERSHAM, happening, a few months after, to lofe their principal (who was always one of a con-

:)

PRIOR of BATH ; who, Mr. BATTELY adds, died the greateft part of a century before, that is, in 1412.—

It is to be lamented, that monaftic anti-quities are fo often overfhadowed by fuch a cloud of uncertainty :—but the ftory of the SISTERS feems to clear up the doubt of who this JOHN THE ABBOT was ; and may dif-pofe the Antiquarian, to reinftate JOHN DE SAINT CLAIR, in the high dignity he is faid to have formerly enjoyed.—

fiderable

fiderable family) the ABBOT of SAINT AUGUSTIN, perceiving her fixed in her fcheme of life, procured her to be named the Lady ABBESS of it.

ISABELLA, who had never as yet been feparated from her fifter, would, on this occafion, moft willingly have taken the veil.—"The fame roof," fays fhe, " hath ever hitherto covered us, " —the fame have been our wifhes,— " the fame our purfuits ;—the grave " hath divided us from thofe, who " taught us the amiablenefs of friend- " fhip,—and fhall alone divide us " from one another !"—

—The ABBOT was much hurt by this declaration of his niece.—He defired her to banifh from her thought, fuch a refolution ;—and fail- ed not to intimate to her, that FRANCES, having devoted herfelf to the

the cloyſter, ſhe remained the only ſupport of the family of SAINT CLAIR; that her virtues ſhould rather embelliſh ſociety, than be loſt within the walls of a monaſtery;—and wiſhed ſhe would, by accepting ſome alliance of ſuitable rank and fortune, rather permit thoſe accompliſhments to be ſeen by the world, which ſhe ſought to hide in oblivion.—

FRANCES, on her part, however ſhe was charmed with this teſtimony of her ſiſter's affection, joined in ſentiment with her uncle,—expreſſing to her, how much happier ſhe ſhould be, to ſee her ſettle herſelf by marriage, and imitate the good life, and example of their excellent mother.—

" I am not, you know," ſays ſhe, " by the religious office I fill, tied
" down

" down to all thofe rules, which muft
" of courfe be impofed on you;—my
" liberty remains;—we fhall have
" conftant opportunities of continu-
" ing that intercourfe of love, our
" hearts fo mutually defire.—It will
" be the higheft pleafure to me, to
" fee you united to a man worthy
" your choice;—preferving in our
" father's caftle, that hofpitality, for
" which it hath fo long been famed;
" —and whenever you fhall wifh to
" make a fhort retreat from the buf-
" tle of the world, our holy houfe
" will afford you a peaceable afy-
" lum."—

—It was not but with great difficulty, nor even till much time after,
that, by the repeated folicitations of
FRANCES, and her uncle, ISABELLA
was prevailed on to relinquifh en-
tirely,

tirely, her intentions of entering on a monaſtic life.—She reſided for ſome time, in her father's venerable old manſion on the MEDWAY, accompanied by a widowed aunt, her father's ſiſter;—who, at intervals, attended her on viſits to FRANCES,—and alſo, at particular ſeaſons, to the ABBOT, at his houſe, which was a noble building, adjoining to the monaſtery of SAINT AUGUSTIN.

—It was in one of theſe viſits to her uncle, that ſhe became acquainted with HENRY DE BELVILLE, between whoſe father and the ABBOT, there had long ſubſiſted a moſt firm friendſhip.—He was of good birth, though much inferior to ISABELLA in fortune; his father's eſtate having greatly ſuffered in the confuſion of thoſe turbulent times.—

BELVILLE

BELVILLE was now in his twenty-ninth year;—his figure was graceful, and manly,—and, to a difposition as amiable as his perfon, was joined an underftanding both quick and ftrong, and which had been improved by the moft extenfive education, that the fafhion of the age allowed.—He had been fent to travel over EUROPE,—had refided in feveral of its principal courts;—and was now on his return from a fhort expedition into FRANCE, —and had ftopped at CANTERBURY, to pay his refpects to the ABBOT, and to deliver him certain letters with which he had been charged.—

BELVILLE, on his firft return to ENGLAND, a few years previous to the prefent period, had been honoured by the patronage of RICHARD Duke of GLOUCESTER; near whofe

7   perfon,

perfon he held an employment, which
could not long difpenfe with his ab-
.fence;—for that prince, being now
mounted on the throne of ENGLAND,
the whole nation was thrown into an
hoftile ftate.—

It will not be wondered at, if after
BELVILLE and ISABELLA had been a
few days together, their mutual accomplifhments, and their mutual defire to pleafe, fhould have made them
much charmed with one another.—
—BELVILLE felt himfelf enamoured
of his fair companion,—and had the
fatisfaction to perceive, that his attention to her was not thrown away.
—Though he took leave, after a fhort
time, to go to LONDON, yet he found
an excufe for returning very foon;
—and having reafon to think he
had made a favourable impreffion

on

on ISABELLA, did not long hesitate to propose himself to her, as one who would be happy to pass his life, in the society of so engaging a wo-man.—His offer was not less pleasing to ISABELLA, than it was to her uncle, and FRANCES;—the latter of whom agreed to give up to her sister, her right in the castle of SAINT CLAIR, where it was proposed they should reside.—

—Every thing was preparing for their nuptials;—and nothing could wear a fairer face of prosperity, than did this purposed union of true and disinterested affection.—But the suc-cessful progress that the arms of HENRY OF RICHMOND, now made in the kingdom, had obliged RICH-ARD to oppose them with his utmost force, and to summon all his servants

to

to attend his camp; amongſt whom, as I before mentioned, was the intended bridegroom ; who at this time would moſt willingly have waved the ſervice, had not his own nice ſenſe of honour, and his zeal for his royal maſter, overcome every private motive.—

—Were I to follow cloſely, the manuſcript from whence the ſubſtance of this ſtory is drawn, it would lead me into ſome of the hiſtorical tranſactions of thoſe times, which are already ſufficiently known;—only it is worthy of being remembered, that there are encomiums beſtowed on the character, and perſon of RICHARD ; upon both of which, hiſtorians have thrown ſo much deformity.—I ſhall therefore paſs over thoſe circumſtances, which are foreign to my

VOL. II.   K   ſubjeet,

fubject; and only obferve, that the unfortunate BELVILLE was amongft
thofe of the king's followers, who
fhared their royal mafter's fate in
BOSWORTH FIELD. — He was near
RICHARD in great part of the battle,
and was alfo a witnefs of his death;
—and his own horfe being killed under him, either by the fall, or by being
trampled on in the confufion, his thigh
was broken; and, after RICHMOND's
party had obtained the victory, this
gallant youth was carried, with feveral others wounded, into LEICESTER,
—where, his rank being known, he
was lodged in a monaftery of BLACK
FRIARS, in that city.

—His page, BERTRAM, who had
ferved him from his infancy, took
care that every affiftance fhould be
procured him;—but the fever, which

. was

was occafioned by the accident, together with the many bruifes he had
received, neither gave himfelf, or
thofe about him, any other profpect,
but that of approaching death.—

Thofe who contemplate BELVILLE a
few weeks before, in the full vigour of
youth, flattering himfelf with every
expectation of happinefs, that virtue,
fortune, and an union with one of
the lovelieft of women, could prefent
to his imagination;—and now picture
him—ftretched on a poor pallet,—
furrounded by a parcel of mendicant
friars,—his countenance fhrunk and
wan,—and his eyes fixed with humi-
lity, and refignation, on a crucifix
which they held before him,—cannot furely, by the contraft, avoid
dropping a figh, at the fallacy of
human hopes !—

—A little

'—A little before he expired, he defired to be left alone with his PAGE, that he might give him his lateſt orders.——

" BERTRAM," ſays he,—looking wiſtfully on him—" the day that " hath ruined our Sovereign's fortune, " hath blaſted mine !—and that too, " in the moment when it ſhone the " faireſt !—Thou wilt ſoon render " me the laſt of thy faithful ſervices ! " —Let my body reſt with the fa- " thers of this houſe,—and as ſoon " as thou haſt ſeen its due rites per- " formed, ſpeed thee to CANTER- " BURY,—and acquaint the holy AB- " BOT of SAINT AUGUSTIN, with the " bloody event of yeſterday.—Con- " jure him, that he unfold it to my " intended Bride, in ſuch manner

" as

" as his difcretion fhall advife.—Bear
" her this jewel from my finger, in
" token, that my laft thoughts dwelt
" on her;—and tell her, my only
" figh in leaving the world, was for
" the lofing her, whofe virtues fo
" embellifhed it !"—

—The faithful BERTRAM dropped
a tear of affection and gratitude, over
the grave of his gallant mafter;—
and journeying to CANTERBURY with
a burfting heart, prefented himfelf
before the ABBOT, with fuch a countenance, as hardly needed a tongue
to tell his melancholy errand.—

The arrival of BELVILLE'S PAGE,
could not be long a fecret to ISA-
BELLA, who was then at her uncle's;
and whofe mind inftantly foreboded
fome extraordinary event;—though the

K 3

news

news of the battle had not yet reached
that city.——

When Saint Clair was himfelf
fufficiently compofed, to open the
mournful bufinefs to his niece, he
fpared none of that ghoftly comfort,
which a good man would offer on
fuch an occafion ;—though the a-
mount of all that can be faid to
the fons and daughters of affliction,
is no more than this,—that it is our
duty, and our intereft, to bear, with
patience, that which it is not in our
power to alter !—The emotions of nature muft fubfide, before the foothing
voice of reafon can be heard !——

Isabella, after giving way to the
firft tranfports of paffion, affumed a
fortitude, and refignation, which her
piety alone could infpire.—She defired that Bertram might be detained,

tained, two, or three days, at the monaftery,—and as foon as her mind was more fortified, fhe would difpatch him to her fifter FRANCES, whom fhe could then bear to fee with more calmnefs;—and to whom fhe fent the following letter, by the hands of the PAGE.

" Moft beloved Sifter,
" I am plunged from the height of
" imaginary happinefs, into the depth
" of real diftrefs!—The meffenger
" who delivers this, will inform you
" of my fituation,—and to him I re-
" fer you for particulars, which I am
" unable to dwell on.—BELVILLE is
" no more!—All that dream of hap-
" pinefs, which I hoped for, from
" an alliance with that dear, that

K 4
" amiable

" amiable man, is vanifhed in an
" inftant!—and I wake into a world,
" that hath no object for my regard,
" but the affection of my ever tender
" FRANCES!—I fupport my adverfity
" with all the fortitude I can fum-
" mon up;—but Heaven only knows
" the ftruggles of my heart!—From
" the time that the united folicita-
" tions of you, and my Uncle, pre-
" vailed on me (though reluctantly)
" to abfent myfelf from you, my
" foul hath been agitated between
" hope and difappointment!—I will
" truft the fallacy of the world no
" more;—the remainder of my days
" fhall be paffed with you;—and we
" will end life as we began it, in an
" infeparable union.—Your converfe,
" and the folitude of a cloifter, can
" alone

" alone reſtore tranquillity to the
" mind, of your ever faithful, and
" diſconſolate

      " Isabella."

When the Lady Abbess ſaw her
Siſter, ſhe found her ſtill more con-
firmed in her reſolution of entering
on a monaſtic life.—Her Uncle, conceiving it might beſt reſtore a calm
to her troubled ſpirits, no longer op-
poſed it;—and as ſoon as her affairs
were properly adjuſted, and every
thing prepared, ſhe took the veil in
the convent where Frances pre-
ſided.

—Isabella now found in religion, the
only conſolation for her paſt misfortunes;—and though the remembrance
of her beloved Belville, would often
come acroſs her, and ſpread a tem-
porary

porary gloom over her mind,—yet
she constantly strove to dispel it, by
piety and resignation. — The Two
SISTERS enjoyed all that heart-felt
pleasure, which arises from rooted
friendship ;— and, as the effects of
benevolent dispositions operate on
all around, theirs served to com-
municate happiness to all the Sister-
hood.—

The LOUVAIN *Manuscript* informs
us, that after these ladies had passed
near fourteen years in this peaceful
retirement, the ABBESS was seized
with an alarming fever, the effects of
which hung so long upon her, that
they greatly endangered her life.—It
is not difficult to conceive, how severe ISABELLA's sufferings were, in this
dreadful interval of suspense and ap-
prehension, or the anxieties of her
mind,

mind, till her Sifter was reftored to health.—

FRANCES, during her illnefs, had made a private vow to the *Bleſſed Virgin* MARY, that if ſhe recovered, ſhe would ſend ſome coſtly preſent to a chapel, which was confecrated to her, at a little Port, called BRADSTOW, or BROAD-STAIRS, in the Iſle of THANET (part of which chapel is at this day remaining) ;—and in which, her image was eſteemed to work ſuch great miracles, that Pilgrims came from parts very remote, to viſit it ; —and it was held in ſuch veneration, that all ſhips paſſing within ſight of it, are reported to have conſtantly lowered their top-ſails, to ſalute it.—And the feaſt of the INVENTION OF THE HOLY CROSS, which was the third day of MAY, being to be celebrated there,

with

with great folemnity,—her gratitude
for her recovery, and for the fuppofed interceffion of the VIRGIN, determined her to go herfelf at that time,
and fulfil her vow.—

ISABELLA obtained permiffion to
accompany her Sifter in this devout
purpofe ;—and the roads being little
frequented in that age, and a horfe
almoft the only conveyance — they
refolved to put themfelves, with two
attendants, aboard a paffage floop,
that ufually went, at ftated times,
from FEVERSHAM to BROAD-STAIRS,
and other parts along the coaft, between that place and the DOWNS.

—They fet fail in the evening, but
had not been at fea above two hours,
before a violent ftorm arofe.—Every
one who is acquainted with the na-
vigation of this coaft, quite to the
mouth

mouth of the THAMES, knows how difficult it is rendered, by reafon of the many flats, and banks of fand, that obftruct it.——

——The fuddennefs and fury of the ftorm, together with the thunder and lightning that accompanied it, threw a difmay amongft all the paffengers; ——and the mariners, from the op-pofition of the wind and tide, were unable to direct the veffel.——To pur-fue their courfe was impracticable; ——they therefore attempted to fave themfelves, by running in on the fhore, at a little place, called RE-CULVER (which is a fmall village, though of great antiquity, fituate on the border of the Ifle of THANET);—— but the advance of night, and a thick fog, prevented them from dif-cerning exactly, whereabout they

7   were.——

were.—Every endeavour to reach the
shore was frustrated by the storm
driving them from it;—and their sails
being all shattered, a sudden swell of
the sea, bore them quite out of their
direction, and struck the vessel on a
bank of sand, called the HORSE,
that lies a little off from RECUL-
VER.—

—The surprize—the confusion—
and the image of death, that must
naturally rush into the minds of people, who are on the point of being
wrecked,—can only be justly felt, or
described, by those, who have stood
in so dreadful a situation.—Each one
recommended himself to GOD, *and* to his
Tutelar Saint.—The mariners hoisted
out their long boat, as precipitately
as they could;—and that which most
agitated the thoughts of FRANCES

I   and

and ISABELLA, was, the mutual pre-
fervation of each other.—

Scarce was the boat on the furface
of the waves, when every one was
eager to rufh into it;—for it was
certain the veffel muft bulge in a
few hours, — and, to add to the
horror, night advanced.—The Captain, almoft by force, dragged the
Lady ABBESS, and her Sifter, from the
cabin,—and fcarce had he helped the
firft, half dead as fhe was, down the
fide of the fhip, when thofe who were
already in the boat, finding they
muft all perifh, if more got in, pufhed
off inftantly, and rowed towards
fhore,—in fpite of the menaces of
the Captain, who ftood on deck, fup-
porting ISABELLA,—the intreaties of
the ABBESS, who was wild to return,—

turn,—or the cries of the paſſeng
left behind.

—The only faint hope which n
remained to thoſe on board, was, t
the veſſel might poſſibly hold toʒ
ther, till ſome aſſiſtance could be c
tained from the ſhore; which they f
flattered themſelves would come,
caſe the boat reached the land
which it providentially did, thou
with the utmoſt riſk.—Every c
who remained in the veſſel was
ſigned to their fate;—and ſurround
as ISABELLA was, by impending dea
it afforded no ſmall conſolation
her, to think, there was a poſſibili
that her Siſter had eſcaped.

—It was four hours after the a
rival of the boat, before any one du
venture out;—when, the ſtorm abɜ

ng with the departure of the tide,
nd the day being near dawning, a
arge boat put off to the wreck.—
When thofe who went to affift, got
o it, they found all the people on
board, refuged in different places beneath the deck,—great part of which
vas broken away.—ISABELLA had re-
nained in the cabin; one fide of
which was alfo wafhed off, and the
room half filled with water;—fhe
was almoft exhaufted, by the terrors
fhe had fuftained,—the bruifes fhe
had received,—and the extreme cold
in which fhe had fo long fuffered.—
They led her with the utmoft gen-
tlenefs from this wretched place,—
while fhe, all pale, and trembling,
fcarcely comprehended at firft what
they were doing;—yet life feemed to
flufh anew in her countenance, on

hearing that her Sifter was preferved.—

—As foon as they had brought her on fhore, fhe was fupported by feveral women, who were waiting to receive her; and conducted to the houfe where the Lady ABBESS was. — FRANCES, tranfported at the firft fight of her Sifter, ran out to meet ISABELLA,—who, the moment fhe approached, made an effort to fpring forward to her, but funk down, overpowered, into the arms of her attendants.—FRANCES clafped her hand, and in her eager joy, would have uttered fomething, but could only faintly pronounce her name, and fell at her feet in a fwoon.—

ISABELLA was immediately put into bed, and received every affiftance that could be procured;—but her

strength

ſtrength and ſpirits were ſo far ex-
hauſted, by the terror and fatigue,
which her mind and body had under-
gone, and by remaining ſo many
hours in water, that ſhe lived but
till the evening of the following
day.—

FRANCES, though ſtill ſinking from
the ſhock and agitation of the preceding night, forgot, in her attention
to her Siſter, her own ſufferings.—
She never ſtirred from her bedſide,—
and often accuſed herſelf, as being the
fatal cauſe of all that had befallen her,
by ſuffering her attendance in this
expedition.—ISABELLA chid her for
thinking ſo,—declaring, it was the
will of Heaven, to which ſhe patiently
ſubmitted.—" Though we came into
" the world together," ſays ſhe, " yet
" as we were not deſtined to periſh

" toge-

" together,—a time muſt inevitably
" have come, when death would have
" diſſolved our union.—I rejoice that
" I am not the ſurvivor.—I die,
" where I have ever wiſhed to live,
" in the arms of the moſt beloved of
" Siſters.—Pray for the repoſe of my
" ſoul;—and lay me in the tomb
" which you have allotted to be your
" own — that one grave may in
" death hold our Remains, who in
" life had but one heart."

The loſs of ISABELLA plunged the
lady ABBESS into that deep diſtreſs,
which minds, formed like her's, with
the nobleſt ſentiments of tenderneſs,
and benevolence, muſt, on ſuch a
trial, inevitably feel.—She cauſed the
body of her unfortunate Siſter to be
tranſported in ſolemnity, to their convent;—where, after it had been ex-

poſed

pofed with accuftomed rites, it was
depofited, with every mark of refpect,
in a vault, on one fide of the fhrine
of SAINT BENEDICT,—bedewed with
tears of the moft heart-felt forrow,
dropped from the eyes of all the
Sifterhood.—

—When time and reflection had
fomewhat calmed her affliction,
FRANCES failed not to tranfmit, by
the hands of her Confeffor, (her uncle,
the ABBOT, having been fometime
dead *) her intended offering to the
Virgin

---

* This circumftance feems fully to decide the point of JOHN DE SAINT CLAIR
being the ABBOT, whofe family name is
loft in all the chronicles of SAINT AU-
GUSTIN's monaftery.—Mr. BATTELY tells
us, that JOHN THE ABBOT died in 1497;

and

Virgin of BROAD-STAIRS,——accompanied by a donation of twelve maſſes, to be ſaid for the repoſe of ISABELLA's ſoul.——And ſoon after, to perpetuate the memory of her Siſter,—— as well as to direct mariners in their courſe,—that they might eſcape the ſad calamity herſelf had ſo fatally experienced, — ſhe cauſed an ancient church that ſtood on a riſing ground juſt above the village of RECULVER, and which was greatly fallen into decay, to be reſtored, and much enlarged, — and erected *Two Spiral Towers* at the end thereof; — the which ſhe directed ſhould be called

and the connexion this ſtory has with the battle of BOSWORTH FIELD, which was fought in 1485, fixes the preſent period to be in ſome part of the year 1500.

THE

THE SISTERS;—and to this day it retains the name, and is a fea-mark of great utility.—

In lefs than seven years, the whole church was completed; which fhe endowed very liberally, by a grant out of her own fortune;—and ordained, that there fhould be celebrated one folemn mafs, *on the firft day* of every month (the wreck having happened on the *firft of May*); and that a perpetual litany fhould be fung, for the eternal peace of the departed ISABELLA.—

She lived to fee this her Will executed,—as well as to beftow many other charitable donations,—not only on the convent over which fhe prefided,—but on feveral other religious inftitutions;—and was, from her amiable

able

able character, and pious example, beloved, and refpected to the laft hour of her life.——

She furvived ISABELLA eleven years, and died moft fincerely, and defervedly lamented, towards the end of the year 1512.——

Her Remains, purfuant to her own defire, were depofited by the fide of thofe of her Sifter, with all that folemnity due to her high rank, and office. —— A monument was erected near to the place, where they were interred, with their figures kneeling, hand in hand, before a crofs,—and beneath it, a plate of brafs, recording their unfhaken friendfhip.——

——Faithful,—congenial fpirits !—in whatfoever worlds ye refide, peace be your lot!—as virtue was your portion

tion here!—Long, long may this memorial of your love remain!—to guide the dubious veffel in its courfe, and make your names bleft by the wanderers of the deep!—

SHIP

SHIP-NEWS.

THERE rarely paffed a day, during my ftay at MARGATE, of
which I did not fpend fome portion
in the fociety of CLERMONT, and his
fifter.—On calling upon them this
afternoon, I thought every body's
countenance faluted me, with more
than its wonted good-humour.—It is
a circumftance that ever gives one
the moft pleafant feelings.

—As I, in turn, addreffed my in-
quiries to MARIANNE, I perceived
a blufh on her cheek,—together with
a little apparent hurry of fpirits.—
She was moving about the room in
queft of fomething,—and prefently
went up ftairs—either to look for a fan,
which fhe had in her pocket—or her
work-bag,

work-bag, which *hung upon her arm,*
—though more probably to give
AMELIA an opportunity of fpeaking
with me.

—If I had not known, faid that
Lady, that you were to dine to-day
at SAINT LAURINCE, I fhould certainly have fent you a fummons;—for
I was impatient to tell you, that
both my young friend, and myfelf,
have received letters, this morning,
from STERLING, who is got to IRE-
LAND.—Mine breathes the effufion of
a grateful mind, kindly approving,
and applauding, the part I have acted;
—MARIANNE's I have kept in my
pocket, for your perufal;—and I now
think nothing more can difturb an
union, in which I confefs myfelf interefted, with the fondeft feelings of a
mother.—But read the letter.—

7   " I feize

" I feize the earlieft moment, of
" informing my deareft Girl, of my
" fafe arrival in IRELAND,—where I
" hope I fhall foon complete my bufi-
" nefs—and then fet my fails to-
" ward ENGLAND, whither all my
" thoughts, and wifhes, are flown be-
" fore me.—I have a thoufand things
" to fay to you,—but time will only
" allow me to tell you, that your's
" and AMELIA's letters, reached me
" at the CAPE. — Heavens! — how
" was I tortured, when I learned whom
" it was, that had fo cruelly,—though
" fo unfuccefsfully,—tampered with
" our feelings!—Poor EDMUND!—
" but his name fhall never again be
" mentioned;—he cannot be more
" feverely punifhed, than to reflect,
" that in the exigencies of future
" life, he hath deprived himfelf,

for

"for ever, of the comfort and affec-
"tion of fuch a fifter!—Yourfelf,
"and your faithful protectrefs, have
"been the guardians of my happi-
"nefs.—But I hope I have many
"years before me, to pay that debt,
"which my heart fo gratefully avows;
"—though the debts of *Senfibility*,
"and of *Love*, are the reverfe of all
"others,—for, in the intercourfe of
"feeling minds, every attempt to *dif-*
"*charge* them, proves but the means
"to *increafe* them!—Be this, my
"deareft MARIANNE, the commerce
"of our lives!—I muft now bid you
"adieu,—that I may, before the de-
"parture of the poft, exprefs to your
"generous friend, how much her
"conduct hath obliged me.—I wait
"the moment with impatience, when

"my

" my lips can better affure you, how
" much I am for ever

" Your's, &c.

" STERLING."

AMELIA, all the while I was reading the letter, was wiping away a
tear, — and CLERMONT brufhed off
half a dozen that had filently flipt
from his eyes.

—Well, fays he, when I had finifhed it,—what think you now of
the young man?—If his heart does
not hang in the right place, I will
never have an opinion of my own,
while I breathe.—I have not a doubt,
but he will make my *adopted niece*, a
fenfible, manly, and affectionate hufband.—You fmile at my calling her
fo;—but I muft own to you, that I
wifh

wish to imbibe every partiality of my
sister's;—and MARIANNE is such a
natural, engaging character, that to
know her well, and not be partial to
her, would be an impossibility.—
But, my old acquaintance, I have
something more to say to you on this
subject, for EMILY vows that no one
but yourself, shall perform the matri-
monial ceremony;—and she is confident that you are too much interested
for her friend, to have any objection.—

—She may be assured, I can have
none.—There is so much real satisfaction in being *intentionally*, or even
officially, an instrument to the happy
union of others, that I feel an obli-
gation to any one, who suggests to
me the means of becoming so.—My
precarious health, continued I, would
never

never allow me to execute the calls of my profeſſion, where the duty was conſiderable;—nor my principles, to accept *a truſt*, which I felt myſelf *unable to perform*,—yet its offices have been ever ready to the claims of humanity, or of friendſhip.—And to ſay truth, Madam, in the one you now ſolicit, I am as lucky a perſon as you could poſſibly apply to,—for I never married but three couple ;—and though ſeveral years have ſince elapſed, yet I never meet them, without ſeeing a ſmile on their countenances, and receiving, from both ſides, a repetition of their thanks ;—and this cordial acknowledgment, charms me the more in one of them, who was my intimate at College ; as his happineſs can only ariſe from the great ſuperiority of his mind, to the narrowneſs rownefs of his fortune ;—for with the education and deportment of a gentleman, and a fcholar, —and under the difficulties, which the providing for five children muft create, — he had never fufficient intereft to procure a living,—yet cheerfully goes through the daily, laborious duty of an extenfive, and populous parifh, which he fuftains with the confcientioufnefs of an apoftle, for feventy pounds a year; while his dignified rector, who rarely vifits the place, receives more than fix times that fum from it !—

It is to be lamented, refumed CLERMONT, that the preferments of the church are not more equally divided ;—many have too much,—and the greater part of the clergy, far too little ;—and, though I would not doubt, but that in the difposal of the good things of this world, merit hath often its fhare; yet the only true paffport to the obtaining them, is, what you call in this country, *connexion*.—Without the aid of a patron who has intereft, mere merit ftands but little chance of being noticed;— and a man, even with the fhining virtues of your friend, may continue to ftarve on a curacy, all the days of his life.—

—But my good Sir, allow me one word more on the fubject—No one more truly refpects the clergy than myfelf, when their doctrine, and their characters, illuftrate each other—nay, I firmly believe, that mankind are univerfally difpofed to reverence their function;—but, bred a merchant,— and accuftomed to look daily, on the

debtor

debtor and creditor fide of my books,
—and to have a conftant eye on the
balance of both,—I am at a lofs to
guefs what kind of confcientious balance fome of your Dignitaries ftrike,
who undertake the *cure of fouls*, yet
fo far from affording them their fa-
lutary aid, do not even know either
them, or their *diforders*. — You will
excufe me, my friend,—but it feems
to be juft the cafe of an apothecary,
who fhould charge his *own attendance*,
yet entruft all his patients to the fole
infpection of his *journeyman*.—

Prithee, *how can you account* for this
total negligence ? or, for what is almoft as culpable,—the being fo little
of the vigilant fhepherd, as only to
look after the *flock* in the time of
fheering ?—

—I am inclined to hope, faid I,

for

for the honour of my profeſſion, that
this is not in general the caſe; and
ſhall therefore only reply to you, that
as it is a queſtion not ſo proper to be
anſwered by proxy, I would rather
leave its deciſion to thoſe whom it
may concern.——

    This, however, you may depend on
——that it is *to be accounted for.——*✕

THE

ALL the crowned heads of the MAR-
GATE drama would, unqueftiona-
bly, take it amifs, fhould they be paffed over in filence.—Though it is my
wifh to *pleafe* all,—I poffefs a defire
equally ftrong to *offend* none,—and
leaft of all, thofe. who exert their
abilities for the entertainment of
others.—Though the Kings,—Lords,
—and Commons,—in their theatrical
barn affembled, convey fuch confufed
ideas of the perfonages they reprefent,
that they become caricatures inftead
of charaƈters ;—nor do they probably,
in general aim at any thing more,—
for there is ufually fuch a poverty, and
laughable diftrefs, running through the
whole performance, as renders Comedy

M 3   extremely

extremely ridiculous, and Tragedy truly comical.——

Some ladies of AMELIA's acquaintance, having, through humanity, patronized one of the poor players, befpoke HAMLET,——and exerted their intereft to fill the houfe—it being for the *benefit* of the GHOST, and his wife.

CLERMONT and I were folicited to be of the party;—but the Theatre being much crowded, I found myfelf unable to fuftain the heat of it.—— My friend and I, therefore, before the curtain drew up, retired behind the fcenes;—and indeed, when we were got there, perceived but little probability, that it would draw up the whole evening,—for furely never was beheld fuch a fcene of confufion, as then appeared, in what ferved both

for

for their general dreſſing-room, and green-room.—

The centinels, who were to mount guard before the palace of the *Royal* DANE, for want of having any uniform in the wardrobe, had borrowed a couple of ſailors jackets.—HORATIO was ſtriding about in a monſtrous rage,—declaring he would not act, becauſe his own benefit had been unjuſtly put back.—The manager, who was corpulent enough to have perſonated FALSTAFF, even almoſt without ſtuffing, — apparelled as young HAMLET, was in no leſs a paſſion too,—damning the GHOST's *blood* for being in liquor,—who, as well as his wife, had, on the credit of the many tickets which were taken, given way, through exceſs of joy, at dinner, to an indulgence they ſhould more pru-

dently

dently have poftponed till night.—
The GHOST had little to fay in his
defence, — but his lady, now the
Queen Mother,—fat royally robed on a
joint-ftool,—and whilft fhe was dab-
bing the laft colouring on her cheeks,
hickupped, with much brevity, their
mutual apology.—Nor did the diftrefs end here—a fmith was fent for
to break open OPHELIA's *coffin*,—
which ferving as a travelling trunk
to this itinerant company, the GHOST's
helmet, POLONIUS's *wig*, together with
fome of the DANISH *regalia*, were
lodged within it ;—and the manager,
having alfo depofited with them a
half anchor of *run fpirits*, had fo
carefully put away the key, that in
the hurry it could not be found,—
fo that the mufic kept playing *roaft
beef*, and every popular tune they
could

could think on, to amufe the impatient audience, who knew nothing of the woeful diforder that reigned behind.

—The performance was fuch as might naturally be fuppofed from the fituation and temper of the *Dramatis Perfonæ.*—The GHOST compofed himfelf far better than I expected,—except, that in the clofet fcene, he exerted more violence than became his character,—and rufhing in, too eagerly, dropped his coat of mail which was accidentally untied.—However, as his fhirt happened to be clean, he might pafs in it full as well for an inhabitant of the other world, as he did in his old leathern armour.

—OPHELIA's dirty filk gown, had been deftined for a woman far more flender than herfelf,—on which account

count, the robings pinned almoft at her hips, and left her in great difficulties to form a convenient ſtomacher.—Neither ſhe, nor the QUEEN could raiſe a pair of gloves,—and the latter having ſcalded her arm, by taking off a pot from the fire, was compelled to appear with it bound round with old linen, — which, in truth but *ill became the majeſty of* DENMARK.—The play was received with great indulgence, and excited much more mirth, than it did either terror, or pity.——

I have often conſidered myſelf, when behind the ſcenes of more reſpectable theatres, to be in the ſituation of thoſe who are in reality about ſuch elevated characters in life, as on the ſtage are only perſonated.—They ſtand in a very different point of view.

to thofe who obferve them near, when they are not acting their parts,—and who fee what poor, flimfy materials contribute to deck them out, as objects for the public eye!

—It is of much moment, on which fide of the curtain we contemplate either men, or things!—

It were next to impoffible to fee fuch noble fcenes, as are interfperfed in this whimfical tragedy, blundered through, and converted to farce, without their exciting a hearty laugh;—and yet, on the beft regulated theatres, how few are there who can fupport a fine drawn character chaftly, and admirably throughout?—The dignified fcenes of the *Tragic Mufe*, befides an harmonious voice and ear, fuperadded to very many perfonal accomplifhments in the player, demand

strong

ftrong judgment, and delicate feelings,—and fuch who poffefs this af-
femblage of endowments (a few ex-
ceptions allowed) rarely choofe to ex-
pofe their talents in a fituation of this
nature,—Should any future fafhion
render the profeffion eligible, there
would be found, with fuch advantages, no myftery in it,—nor would
the ftage feel the want of as great or-
naments, as it hath hitherto ever
boafted.—The fame argument muft
inevitably appear juft, with refpect to
the *lighter fcenes* of the drama;—it
being difficult for an actor, without
the aid of a very fuperior genius, to
delineate, with eafe, and propriety,
manners which he is not *familiarized*
to himfelf.—Hence it is, that the
characters of genteel comedy, are thofe
which in general fuffer the moft in
repre-

reprefentation, — while the ftrong-
marked features of common life,
rarely fail of receiving their due colouring.—

As CLERMONT and I, between the
play and the farce, were debating
thefe matters, on an old form, which
ten minutes before had conftituted
the *Throne* of DENMARK—Our neigh-
bours, fays my friend, underftand
this bufinefs better ;—their natural
vivacity, and habitual politenefs, give
them great advantages on the ftage,
—and their's is the only ftage I have
feen, where their people of rank and
fafhion are perfectly well perfonated.
—When they get into their bufkins,
I own there is far more declamation,
than I think natural—but their dramatic compofitions are excellent.—
I know not whether a long abfence

from

.from the ENGLISH theatre, and a fre-
.quent attendance on the FRENCH one,
.hath vitiated my judgment,—but I
confefs, I love a tragedy that ends
happily, and where the ftruggles of
virtue are crowned with triumph.—
Pity is a more pleafing exercife of
the human mind, than *terror!*—Scenes
of this kind, I have ever obferved, are
honoured with the moft tears;—and
tears are the plaudits of unerring
nature!—A judicious writer will deeply intereft the paffions—awaken fenfibility,—and penetrate every avenue
to the heart, without the aid of either
murder, or of death;—which, by being
made too familiar to our fight, foon
lofe the effect they fhould infpire.—
To fpeak plainly, I think we have
dealt rather too largely in daggers,
and poifon, on this fide of the water
—I hate

—I hate a fifth act, which, as this of to-night, makes the ftage like the fhop of a *carcafe butcher*.—If we had our eye a little more on the FRENCH theatre, I can never believe we fhould write the worfe for it.—

—For Heaven's fake, my good friend, cried I, forbear any parallel!—Ever live *well* with thofe you muft live *with*;—people do not always give up opinion with good-humour. —The great fcenes of SHAKESPEARE,— which no pen hath hitherto either *rivalled*, or *approached*,—will, I hope, ever live on our ftage, in fpite of fome few abfurd ones with which they are intermixed. — You muft confi- der this PRODIGY of NATURE, as born in an age, when the rules of dramatic writing were but little ftu- died, even in the moft polifhed na-

I   tions.—

·tions.—Many of his fucceffors, who copied his faults, though unable to imitate his beauties, may in truth, afford you an ample field for criticifm —However, to pacify your fpirit, allow me to fay, that fince the period when you left ENGLAND, we have had our obligations to the FRENCH theatre,—and very many pieces, whofe grofs *Abfurdities* did not fhock our wife grand-fathers,—nor whofe great *Immodefty* put our virtuous grand-mothers out of countenance,—would not, I affure you, now be allowed an audience.—

Step by ftep, we fhall draw nearer to truth,—and it is no fmall advance toward *Tafte* and *Nature*,—to have got rid of *Indecency*, and *Improbability*.

EDUCATION.

CLERMONT poſſeſſes one of the beſt of hearts, together with an excellent underſtanding, much improved by books, yet far more by a long knowledge of the world—but is at the ſame time, ſo ſettled in his opinions, that he will not readily give up a point.——

——After our return from the play, no ſooner was the ſupper-cloth removed, than he entered again on the topic of dramatic writing; which led him naturally enough, in defence of what he had before urged on that head, to aſcribe much of our notions, on this ſubject, to the *Prejudices of Education*; —which being allowed by both of us, all the weight they neceſſarily muſt

have, like moſt diſputants we ſoon
got a little wide of the mark from
whence we ſtarted, and inſenſibly
found ourſelves on new ground—
nay, on the very ground from whence
thoſe *Prejudices* ſpring.

What we meet with every day,
continued CLERMONT, is ſo familiarized to us, that it paſſes without
making the ſmalleſt impreſſion, —
the mind rarely pauſes to conſider it ;
—and hence many a local error, or
abſurdity, is ſtill perſevered in—Now
I have myſelf been ſo long an Alien
from my own country, and thereby
become a citizen of the world, that
I may poſſibly, from the above cauſe
(you will excuſe me, my friend) view
many things that relate to modern
education, in a very different light to
yourſelf.

My

My own obfervations, faid I, will
lead me to affent readily, to the truth
of what you have been afferting,
" That the youth of moft countries
" in EUROPE, appear to be much
" earlier fafhioned to the world, than
" our own ;"—that is, they attain the
manners, and deportment of men, at
a much earlier period.—Accuftomed
to a conftant intercourfe with ladies,
they cultivate that habitual attention
and politenefs, which is not eafily acquired in reclufe feminaries, folely
devoted to learning—nor, indeed, do
they at the fame time feem deficient
either in ufeful, or ornamental fcience
—but, like fkilful gardeners, make
the moft of the foil, and fpread out
both fruit, and flowers, in the fame
feafon.—Whether they may be fo
deep grounded in GREEK and LATIN,

I leave

I leave to the decifion of our *Heads of Houfes* — being myfelf a traveller only in purfuit of NATURE;—and if in any of my SKETCHES, I occafionally introduce the effects of ART, it is merely as a back-ground, to contraft, and throw forward, the great object I aim to delineate.——

As to your *Heads of Houfes*, replied CLERMONT, they would decide it againft all EUROPE, without taking one turn round their QUADRANGLE, to debate the queftion.——I would, how-ever, on no account, be underftood to depreciate a profound knowledge in either of thofe languages;—you may recollect, when we were together at the Univerfity, I was efteemed a good proficient in both—yet, though they have pleafurably filled up many parts of my life, I cannot fay that

the

the profit they have been of to me, has been in the fmalleft degree *adequate* to the wafte of years that elapfed in attaining them;—and of years—be it remembered—that return no more! —I fee no reafon why they might not be acquired in a far fhorter time —How little a fpace makes us maf-ters, of not only one, but of many of the tongues of EUROPE?—nay, much deeper mafters too, than moft of us ever become of the others?—I cannot but think our fyftem of education, rather calculated for beings who could infure *half a century* of longer exiftence, than is commonly allotted to the race of man.—A *fourth part* of the very longeft life,—and a *full half* of what the generality of mankind actually know, is almoft folely appropriated to the being able

to

to read, and conftrue, two dead
languages, that have been more than
a thoufand years out of ufe;—and,
though I may be thought to merit
being burnt for a *Heretic*, I muft afk
you, what is the fum of knowledge
which they convey?—and to which
this large portion of our days is devoted?—Of the books that are put
into our hands, the far greater part
are the Poets, who inftruct us in the
extravagant fyftem of *Ancient Mythology*—than which human folly never
invented any thing, fo compleatly abfurd,—fo compleatly vitious.—The
boy has no fooner got grounded in
his catechifm, than he is introduced
to a familiarity with the Heathen
Divinities, male and female!—and
fuch a fet of ragamuffins they are, as
hardly ever difgraced the earth;—unjuft,—

juft,—libidinous,—revengeful,—with more than mortal failings, and with more than mortal paffions,—fpreading their vices through all regions, and peopling half the globe with their baftard progeny!—

Downright *Herefy* indeed! cried I. —But downright truth, neverthelefs, refumed my old friend;—nor need I prove it, by citing examples which every fchool-boy hath his head crammed with:—Only as one inftance, let us take the character of JUPITER, *the father of all the gods*;—married to his own fifter,—filling heaven and earth with his enormous debaucheries,—ufing his omnipotence only to accomplifh his abandoned purpofes, —defcending in a fhower of gold to ravifh DANAE, — reverfing even the laws of Nature,—transforming him-

felf

felf into an *Eagle*, for GANYMEDE,—
into a *Bull*, to indulge his paffion for
EUROPA,—and into a *Swan*, to com-
mit a rape on LEDA — who, in confequence of her criminal intercourfe,
with the Thunderer of OLYMPUS, is
ordained to lay *a couple of eggs*, from
which fhe *hatches* CASTOR, and POL-
LUX, and their Two Sifters !—

Such are fome of the outlines that
diftinguifh JOVE himfelf !—and fuch
are the *firft rudiments* of inftruction
that are poured into the youthful
mind !—So that almoft every lad who
happens to depart this life, before he
goes to the Univerfity, leaves the
world with very little other knowledge, than this incoherent jargon
which hath infulted his underftanding !—

—I much doubt, replied I, whether

ther their Reverences have ever confi-
dered this point,—and I muft freely
own, that there is much plaufibility
in what you have faid.—We are all
certain, that our *firft impreffions* are
thofe which are retained the longeft,
and are with the utmoft difficulty, if
ever, effaced. — In the morning of
life, when the mind, like an unfold-
ing flower, is fhooting upward,—and
eager after novelty, nourifhes itfelf with
every thing that is planted near it—
it is furely of much moment that it
fhould be *watered* with the *pureft*
fprings!—and reared to TRUTH and
VIRTUE, by the moft unwearied attention!—A knowledge of *Ancient*
Mythology is of great aid, in a later
period of life, to the flights of poetry,
—and hath opened a more fpacious
field to the imitative arts;—but how
far

far thefe fcenes of fiction, and thefe
contemptible immortals you have defcribed, are proper to be the firft acquaintance of our youth, before we
have abilities to feparate *Truth*, from
Allegory,—or what better knowledge
fhould engage that early feafon,—is a
queftion I would wifh to leave undecided,—at leaft, undecided by myfelf.—

As I have been lefs fcrupulous,
refumed CLERMONT, on the fubject,
and as you have already denounced
me a *Heretic*, it will coft but a faggot
extraordinary, if, in the fame caufe,
I advance one ftep farther,—and exprefs to you my doubts, whether alfo
the filling of boys heads, with the
wild ftories of *Ancient Heroes*, who
are held out as fecondary objects of
their attention, might not, on the
whole,

whole, be better omitted. — Diſtinguiſhed examples of magnanimity, and virtue, when diveſted of all legendary nonſenſe, ſhould, unqueſtionably, be ſtrongly impreſſed on their memories,—but the generality of thoſe who have deſcended to our times, under the denomination of HEROES, have been ſuch as have acquired that title, from their unjuſt conqueſts, and lawleſs devaſtations. —It is to be lamented, that the world hath implicitly affixed ſo much imaginary repute to their names, that, trained up in their *ſplendid deluſions*, young people, I fear, much too often, read the ſad annals they have ſtained with blood, without feeling that laudable indignation, for the violated rights of humanity, which, but for the *impoſitions* of Education, Nature

ture would excite in their bosoms.——
I freely own, I have so little veneration for this class of Beings, that I
feel a satisfaction whenever their ti-
tles are depreciated;——and am happy
to find, that there are people in the
world bold enough to disgrace daily,
even the name of a CÆSAR——by
making it the appellation of a sni-
velling *Lap Dog,* or a little *Negro
Slave* in a WEST INDIAN family.——

As this subject hath engaged our
thoughts, I cannot quit it, without
expressing my wonder, that in our
eager and long pursuits of *dead languages,* so little attention is paid to
the being correct, and elegant in *our
own*; which, through future years, is
to convey all our sentiments.——Whether we are destined to shine in public as orators, or authors,——or fill with

grace

grace, the ftations of private life—
I am well perfuaded it would be a
moft beneficial part of education,
were our youth accuftomed to read
aloud, and declaim in Englifh. —
Their ear would become habituated
to cadence, — the voice infenfibly
learn to give ftrength, and harmony,
to every period,—and they could not
fail of acquiring a purity of ftyle.—
From this omiffion, how frequently
do we meet with men of great learning, whofe reading gives one pain?
—How often is fine reafoning deli-
vered, without commanding attention?—The offices of the Church per-
formed, without energy, — and the
debates of the Senate, divefted of
that elocution, which always fo power-
fully graces both the fpeaker, and
the argument?

On

On this head, returned I, I totally join with you.—You muſt remember Dr. Classic, the ſenior fellow of our college;—no man *deeper* in the Greek and Roman tongues,—no man *ſhallower* in his own;—he could write twenty pages of Ciceronian Latin, —but talked English as coarſely as a waſherwoman,—and read it in a worſe tone than the bellman.—

—I am rather ſurprized, brother, ſays Amelia, that in your criticiſm on modern education, the mode of training up young ladies, ſhould have eſcaped your remarks,—in which *Fiddlers* and *Dancing-maſters* are conſidered as the ſupreme object of attention; and may fairly diſpute the time with your Greek and Latin.—

Why truly, Madam, replied Clermont, the fine parts which Nature hath

hath beſtowed on your ſex, are not
always, I muſt confeſs, cultivated in
the moſt advantageous manner ;—and
perhaps, too much ſtreſs is laid on
thoſe external accompliſhments, which,
in a very few years, are neglected,
even by · thoſe, who have attained
them with ſo much time and aſſi-
duity!—But women, my dear EMILY,
who poſſeſs the good ſenſe you are
miſtreſs of, perceive the *Inſufficiency*
of faſhion, and of themſelves rectify
its *Errors.*—

—I am much obliged to you for
your compliment, brother ; and hope,
for the credit of our ſex, that the ſentiments you entertain of us, are juſt.
—I have ever wiſhed my young friend
here to *follow,* but not *ſacrifice* to faſhion.—External accompliſhments are

7   great

great aids to personal charms,—but beauty, if not affifted by fomething more, hath rarely fufficient power to maintain long the conqueft it hath made.—It is only when united with the graces of the mind, that its victory becomes complete!—The Friend, —the Companion,—and the Miftrefs, —then join to bind faft the chaplet of Love,—and the empire of domeftic happinefs, is founded not in *paffion*, but in the *Heart*!—But our candles are almoft burnt out, and it is time, I think, to withdraw.—

I did not apprehend, Madam, faid I (looking at my watch, and perceiving it was paft twelve) that we had trefpaffed fo much on your hour —but my friend's GODS and HEROES have led us into the fcrape,—and, I

fear,

fear will lead him into a greater one, fhould he ever publifh his opinions to the world.—

As they can never do the world any injury, returned CLERMONT, I am perfectly indifferent about the matter—Whatever oppofes a long eftablifhed cuftom, even though it aims to remove a fuppofed error,—will be fure to have the general voice againft it;—but ingenuous minds, unawed by precedent,—and fearlefs of innovation,—will always hear with candour—and have temper enough to think for themfelves.—ALLEGORY hath placed TRUTH at the bottom of a Well,—on which account fhe is difficult of accefs;—and whenever fhe deigns to vifit us, is a long while emerging.—

We have every reafon to believe

that fpoons were in fome fhape or other, ufed as early as the days of JACOB—but it was near four thou-fand years after, before we found out which was the right way to fix *their handles!*

THE FAREWELL.

AS the exercise and air which I have enjoyed at this place, have contributed to recruit my health, even beyond my utmoſt expectations, I begin now to turn my thoughts toward the Capital;—the family who have made my reſidence here ſo pleaſurable, being alſo ſoon to remove hence. —Indeed, they wait only the arrival of Captain STERLING, who is daily expected; and will in a few days after that event, return back to town— where I hope it will not be long, before I ſhall be called on, to perform the office of uniting the amiable MARIANNE, with her long deſtined huſband.—But there are ever many preli-

minaries

minaries to be fettled on thefe occa-
fions ; and the lawyers always claim
precedence of the church.——

——Be our preliminaries, my dear
JENNY, as fhort as poffible!—I have
given you my heart—which is all I
have to fettle.——

As it will be neceffary, before I
quit MARGATE, to leave a *Card of
Congè* at the door of all my acquaintance, I wifh to take the fame opportunity of dropping one with all my
readers.——By the time it falls into
their hands, we fhall have travelled
almoft through two volumes together, and they will have fpent
hours enough in my company, to
decide whether I am worth their future notice ;—if thofe hours fhould
not have proved unpleafant, we may

probably

probably on fome other ground, meet again, and renew the acquaintance we have now made;—nor can an author, in bidding farewell to his readers, wifh for any circumftance more flattering, than to leave them in a difpofition fo favourable to his intereft.

THE

I HAVE been thefe three days ba-
lancing in my mind, whether I
fhould return to town by land, or
by water.—The great road, however
rich in beautiful profpects, hath no
novelty to me, who have fo frequently travelled it;—and the courfe of the
THAMES, being perfectly new, made
me rather incline to truft the fea;
which, never affecting me with the
leaft ficknefs, is always both pleafant,
and healthful to me.

—But then there is no conveyance
on this element, but the Hoys!—
And what does that fignify?—there
are always merry folks aboard;—and
I have feen them fo many times go
off in fuch high fpirits, that I fhall

not

not diflike to make one among them.
—A crowd affords variety, and is
never unpleasant to me, if I have the
liberty of sitting still in it.—

So this matter was finally adjusted,
and La Pierre sent off to give my
saddle-horses safe conduct to town.

Clermont would see me aboard;
—half Margate thronged the Pier-
Head,—and the deck of the Hoy
seemed already covered with passen-
gers.—The morning was delicious,—
and the sea wore a moft inviting appearance;—so taking leave of my
worthy friend, I ftepped into the veffel,
and feated myself at the ftern, on one
side of the fteerage.

No fooner had we began to push
off, when *a good voyage* was echoed
from an hundred voices at once;—
while, *Do not forget that parcel—*

My

My love to HARRY—*Tell* BETTY *I shall soon be in town*—*Remember me to* JOHN—*Have you got your basket of cold meat?*—*Take care your bonnet does not blow off*—*Be sure give* PEGGY *that letter*;—and a thousand such other mementos, were resounded from various quarters.—

—A fresh gale immediately springing up, we perceived, every five minutes, the coast of MARGATE diminish to our sight;—and indeed we had our eyes, and attention, called another way, by a fleet of more than forty WEST-INDIAMEN, who were all, like ourselves, making for the Port of LONDON, but with an eagerness, far transcending ours, from having traversed such a length of sea to arrive at it.

—I began now to have a little leisure,

to

to furvey the cargo we ourfelves had
on board.—It confifted of a few gentlemen, who, like myfelf, enjoyed a
paffage by fea;—fome decent fhop-
keepers, and their wives, who had
been wafhing off the fummer duft of
LONDON,—and the remainder chiefly
compofed of the fervants of families,
that had left MARGATE, who were
all extremely communicative, and
appeared to have fpent their time in
that happy idlenefs, which fuch an
excurfion from home ufually gives
them.—Every creature at MARGATE
was *monftroufly* polite,—every place
about it *immenfely* pretty,—and the
fmuggled tea moft *extravagantly* cheap.
—I might have picked up *anecdotes*
and *affectation* to have lafted my life,
but the wind kindly blew it half
away, before it could enter my ears.—

Being

Being by this time got into the Mid-Channel, the rolling of the ſhip gave a new turn to matters.—The effects of the breeze, which had hitherto ſo briſkened our courſe, began now to be ſenſibly felt by the greater part of the company;—ſome put on a very ſerious countenance,—ſome turned pale,—others complained of a ſwimming in their head,—others, that every thing moved *under* them,—and it was not long after, before it became very apparent, that every thing alſo moved *within* them;—ſo I ſat very quietly, and gathered up the flaps of my coat,—for I hate to carry away the property of any one.

—They will be all the better for it, thought I, when they get home,—and the ſea not much the worſe.—

As

As we failed by RECULVER, I could not avoid turning a look of love toward THE SISTERS, while my heart in filence, once more bleffed the names of FRANCES and ISABELLA.

There are writers who, fteering the fame courfe that I am, would tell you, that the coaft of ESSEX lay fpread along to the right,—and that of KENT to the left;—which would infer a fuppofition, that the Reader did not know where he was,—and fuch fuppofition muft reflect fome difcredit on an Author.—Now I have in this work already declared, that I meant profeffedly to defcribe nothing; fo fhall leave quite unnoticed; the Bays, Creeks, Inlets of leffer Rivers, and Points of Land, which we paffed,—contenting myfelf with obferving, that our whole courfe, and the

the fine weather that illuminated every object, pictured such a succeffion of beautiful fcenes, as might have furnished a variety of SKETCHES, to thofe who defcribe in *different colours* to myfelf.—

—My aim is not to paint for the *Eye*,—but for the *Heart!*—

The afcending fuch a noble river as the THAMES, cannot but afford to a fpeculative mind, the higheft fatisfaction, from the immenfe traffick which is feen carried on by it,—and the amazing number of fhips, that are failing from the firft commercial city in the world, to convey its arts, and its manufactures to the remote parts of the globe;—while thofe of other nations are pouring in, to enrich us with the advantage of their varied labours, and furnifh us with thofe natural

tural productions denied to our own climate. — One contemplates in the profpect, induftry protected,—ingenuity rewarded,—the wants of life fupplied, — the defires of opulence indulged !—Our enormous Metropolis receives the whole into her port, as the ftomach does its aliments,— which are immediately taken up, and fecreted, by unnumbered ducts, and channels, and thence circulated through ten thoufand veins and arteries, — transfufing national ftrength and wealth, even to the moft remote members.—

After enjoying the beautiful winding of the HOPE, we made a fhort ftop at GRAVESEND, to put fome paffengers afhore, and drop fome goods the mafter had on board ;—by this circumftance, we lay a-long-fide of a

3   Tranfport

Tranſport-veſſel, that was at anchor off that place, and was conveying upwards of *fourſcore* felons to AME-RICA.—Two gentlemen, who had accidentally been my companions in the HOY, had the curioſity to ſtep into the Tranſport; and declared to me at their return, that their humanity was moſt ſenſibly touched, at ſeeing ſo many unfortunate wretches of all ages, from ſixteen, to ſixty, whoſe hardened deportment too ſtrongly teſtified, that even the ſenſe of ſhame, which often outlives the nobler virtues of the mind, in appearance, excited no ſentiment in theirs.

—Heaven protect the country, ſaid I, whither they are going to be tranſplanted !—for they are weeds that muſt diſgrace every ſoil !—It is a melancholy reflection, that neceſſity forces

us

us every year to expel from the kingdom, fuch numbers of our fellow-
creatures, with whom there is no
living but at the rifque of our peace,
and fafety,—and againft whofe fraud
and villany, it requires more art to
fence ourfelves, than againft the moft
favage animals that ravage the world.
—However, as I am going to London, I rejoice to think that there are
at leaft, *fourfcore* fewer rogues in
it, than there were, when I came
away.—

So with this confolation, *in petto*,
we purfued cheerfully, the remainder
of our voyage,—and in about eleven
hours from the time we left Margate, were fafely landed at Wool
Quay.

THE

THE FAMILY-PICTURE.

IT was quite dufk when I got afhore, and the evening being delightfully ferene, I was glad, after fo long a confinement, 'to ftretch my legs, and determined to walk home to my lodgings at the weft end of the town.

—It is a doubt, whether any Capital in EUROPE equals LONDON in populoufnefs, — but it is beyond a doubt, that none vie with it in convenience and cleanlinefs. — I could wifh thofe, who may be inclined to difpute my affertion, would confider the wonderful fecurity in which near a *million* of people are crowded together,—and the equally wonderful manner in which this *million* are fupplied with every thing that neceffity demands,

demands, or extravagance can call for.—The good order preferved in our ftreets by day, — the matchlefs utility and beauty of their illumination by night,—and what is, perhaps, the moft effential of all, the aftonifhing fupply of water which is poured into every private houfe, however fmall, even to profufion!— the fuperflux of which clears all the drains and fewers, and affifts greatly in preferving good air,—health,— and comfort!—

Paris may be fmelt five miles before you arrive at it — . Madrid, ten — and all the great cities of France, and Spain, in proportion: —As to thofe of Italy, the atmofphere which furrounds them, is fo impregnated with *Garlick*, that the nofe cannot eafily analyze the other com-

Vol. II.　　　P　　　pounds

pounds which are overpowered by it;—yet in spite of all the advantages our metropolis may boast, those who are just arrived from the purer air of the country, will, every here, and there, at a short turning, or alley-end, catch many an unsavoury whiff, which they would always wish to get to the windward of.—

—On these occasions I have commonly recourse to my snuff-box; but its contents were unfortunately exhausted, by being liberally offered to some of my companions in the Hoy,— so it occured to me, to call at my old snuff-shop in Covent-Garden, and get it replenished; conceiving I might, at the same time, pick up a little intelligence, of what was stirring in town.—

The shop was lighted up, as usual, and

I   two

two candles ftanding on the counter,—
but the door being bolted, I knocked
twice before I gained admiffion; when
the mafter coming from above ftairs,
complimented me on my return home,
and on the good looks I had brought
back with me.—

I thanked him for his civility,—
and my nofe being become very impatient, I whipped my fnuff-box from
my pocket, and borrowed a hafty pinch,
from the jar he had taken down.

—I thought as he was filling my
box, that his features had more than
their ufual glow of good-nature,—
and at the fame time hearing a female voice above ftairs, accompanied
by a guitar,—I fear, faid I, that I
have called you down from fome con-
vivial meeting—I hate to fufpend
any one's pleafure, even for a mo-

ment—

ment—fo there is my money,—and
now run up again to your friends.—.

You by no means fufpend my
pleafure, replied my tobacconift;—
nay, you will increafe it, by allowing
me to tell you what hath occafioned
it.—It is in truth, a fcene that might
intereft your Feelings.

Two young men, who have for a
great length of time lived with me
under this roof, have endured the
fevere mortification of feeing a worthy
father, whofe talents and ingenuity
might have entitled him to a better
fate, by a feries of misfortunes,
thrown into confinement; and by the
rigour of an unrelenting creditor, detained there for the greater part of
twenty years.—Though their fituation
in life, denied them the power of
refcuing him from his adverfity, yet
they

they have comforted him conftantly by their daily vifits, and fupported both him and his fecond wife, by the labour of their hands ;—ever pouring into his wounded bofom, the balm of filial affection.—An act of grace hath at laft fet the diftreffed parent at liberty,—and they have this evening been to fetch him home from the forlorn fcene of Captivity, which hath worn down his grey hairs.—We have made a little fupper on the occafion ; and had not long finifhed it, when you knocked at the door.—One of his daughters, whofe voice you now hear, is come to welcome his return ; and as all the family have a mufical turn, fhe has taken up a guitar to accompany herfelf.—Nothing can at this moment, exceed the tranfport of the father, after experiencing for fo

P 3   many

many years, the feverity of ill fortune, to find himfelf, at laft, houfed in fecurity under his children's roof.——

——You paint the ftory, returned I, as one who ftrongly fympathized in the general joy.——You might well call it a fcene to *intereft the' Feelings* ;——on my foul, it hath played the deuce with mine,——infomuch, that I would almoft give one eye, to peep through a key-hole with the other, and obtain a glimpfe of thefe happy people, without intruding on their delicious moments.——

Why that, Sir, continued the land-lord, I could gratify you in,——as there can be no breach either of hofpitality, or honour, in exhibiting the merits of one's friends, when their actions may not only bear the view, but claim the applaufe of the world.——

The

The little room where they are, has a glafs folding-door, with a curtain drawn only acrofs the lower half of it,—if you will give yourfelf the trouble to ftep up with me, on the fecond ftairs, you may, unperceived, look over.it, and indulge your curiofity.

—I would not have miffed the fight for all I fhall ever be worth on this fide the grave!—It fhewed me fo lovely a FAMILY-PICTURE, as bid defiance to all the efforts of art ;— even the pencil of a RAPHAEL,—a TITIAN,—or a GUIDO, would have failed in the attempt—for it was drawn, and coloured, by a greater hand ;—by thy inimitable hand, O, NATURE !—who fhalt ever, to the laft page I write, remain the objeft of my adoration !—

—I wifhed a thoufand times, my

dear

dear JENNY, that thy benevolent heart could have enjoyed it with me!—but I will give you fome idea, how the canvafs was difpofed, and your fenfibility will paint the reft.—

Imagine the whole family grouped round the table on which they had fupped,—in full view before me conceive the portrait of the father; whofe features wore the traces of age, and infirmity, poffibly fomewhat ftrengthened by the forrows of life, but whofe countenance was at the fame time brightened by fo placid an eye, as indicated a mind fuperior to them all!—On either fide of him, fat his good fons,—and next to them, his wife, the faithful partner of his afflictions.—Oppofite to her, appeared the vacant chair from whence I had fo abruptly fummoned my conductor,

who

who now ftood by me,—while the daughter whofe voice I had heard from below; and the friendly miftrefs of the houfe, who had prepared them this little entertainment, filled up the remainder of this happy circle.

The daughter was ftill finging to her guitar — they were foothing plaintive notes ;—but my mind was too occupied to attend to founds— it was watching the charaćters which compofed this fingular pićture, and marking attentively the expreffions of cordiality and love, which, during the fong, were fhot from eye to eye.—Often did the good old man caft looks of tranfport on each of his family, one after the other, — then fix his attention on his child, whofe voice was welcoming his return,— while, at intervals, his hands and
eyes

eyes were uplifted, in filent gratitude, to that PROVIDENCE who had, after trials fo fevere, at laft brought him home in peace.——

——As foon as the fong was ended, he beckoned his daughter to approach him;—when, taking her by the arm, he gently pulled her down to his cheek, and hid his face in her neck.——The miftrefs of the houfe now pufhed nearer to him, a glafs of wine, which had been poured out, and had long ftood before him, unregarded, on the table;——he placidly drank it off; and furveying all around him, with a look of meafurelefs contentment, ftretched out his hands on his two fons, who were befide him, which were inftantly preffed in theirs with the utmoft fervor;—— while, in their features, were pictured

tured all thofe delicate emotions of the heart, which NATURE has alone entrufted to the human countenance to exprefs, and which the efforts of language are far too feeble to con- vey.——

——Believe me, my dear JENNY, there was not a dry eye in all the room;—nay, and I might add, on the ftairs neither—for I more than once, obferved my honeft tobacco- nift pafs his hand before his face.——

.——There are tears of *pleafure* as well as tears of *diftrefs!*—the latter are excited by *our own* fufferings,— the former are the involuntary tribute which *Senfibility* pays to *Virtue!*——

I lament, faid I, turning round to my companion, that this picture you have fhewn me, which glows with fo many lovely tints that affection hath

hath fpread over it, fhould be concealed in your little apartment,—it
ought to be exhibited to the Public;
—the view of it might ferve to con-
firm the Good, and fhame the Unfeeling !—Nor could I quit the fcene
I had been contemplating, without
breathing this benediction over it :

—Heaven profper you, children of
Virtue !—nay, and it will profper
you,—for you have given the world
a noble example of filial piety !—
and if loft in its diffipations, it fhould
overlook the unurged claims you
have on it,—yet have you treafured
up in your own bofoms, thofe enviable
feelings of confcious rectitude, which
it never can take from you,—and
which, without hearts like yours,
it hath not in its power to beftow !—

I walked home with fo light and
heedlefs

heedlefs a foot, by having my mind
totally occupied with all I had juft
been fpectator of, that I ran againft
half a dozen pofts, and at leaft treble
as many paffengers.——

I pity, from my foul, the gloomy
temperament of the Satyrift, whofe
delight is to view only the unfavour-
able fide of life.——The imperfections
of humanity may never leave his
fpleen deftitute of a fubject;——yet I
am inclined to believe, for the honour
of PROVIDENCE and NATURE, that
there ever has been a proportionate
degree of benevolence in the world.
——Thofe virtues that moft *adorn*, and
endear fociety, are confined to a limited circle.——Could we fteal in on
the privacies of domeftic life, I am
confident we fhould fee many more
actions and characters to admire, and

7   refpect,

respect, than we are in general inclined to suppose.—

When I arrived at my lodgings,
LA PIERRE met me in the passage
with a countenance that, quicker than
his tongue, told me, all was well—
and that my old horse had performed
the journey—*à merveilles.*

My trusty Valet had made the best
arrangement he could of every thing
in my apartment.—My Sea-Biscuit,
my Capillaire, and my Slippers,
which constitute a part of his evening service, were all placed in order;
—so that I had nothing to do, but to
swallow a mouthful of refreshment,
enquire of him the trivial occurrences of the road, and retire to my
chamber.

—I do not recollect, in all my life,
to have ever passed a more delicious
night;—

night;—for I flept till late the next morning, without the fmalleft inter-ruption,—and arofe in the fineft fpirits imaginable:—Nor will I ever be perfuaded, to this moment, that it was half fo much occafioned by the exercife, and fatigue, of the preced-ing day,—as it was, by my having gone to bed—IN PERFECT GOOD HU-MOUR WITH THE WORLD.

THE END.

www.ingramcontent.com/pod-product-compliance
Lightning Source LLC
Chambersburg PA
CBHW030116030726
47498CB00007B/2411